The Future is a Family - Chapter 11

The Man from Worms

by William F. Arendt

Copyright by PRA, Inc., 1994
3123 W Stolley Park Road
Grand Island, NE 68803 or
P O Box 34392, Omaha, NE 68134
(402)493-0771

ISBN 0-9640235-0-4
Library of Congress
Cataloging in Publication Division
(Number pending)

Printed by Record Printing Company, Cairo NE
Sketches by Marilyn Belschner, Kearney, NE

i

*To the employees of the
Bosselman companies,
both past and present,
who made
this book possible,
and especially
to my family--
Maxine,
Barbara and Chuck,
Fred and Mary.*

Acknowledgements

There are many contributors to this book. First, its instigator, Dr. John H. Easley of Grand Island, without whom nothing would have happened.

Foremost, again, is the Bosselman family, whom I have grown to know and greatly admire. Particularly Maxine and Fred. Their patience with me, their understanding and guidance was a gift I'll always treasure. The late Charles Bosselman, senior brother, also was of great assistance--a man of many talents and strong opinions.

There is a great debt, too, to the many people I interviewed and who contributed photos and/or recollections to make this book possible. At the risk of unduly complicating this Bosselman story, I tried to include most of their observations and stories. Those who were left out were equally contributory; there just wasn't enough room for everyone without getting even more repetitious. For the missing ones: You know who you are and I thank you deeply.

Special thanks also go to the American Trucking Associations, the American Truck Historical Society of Birmingham, Alabama, the Nebraska State Historical Society and the Stuhr Museum of the Prairie Pioneer in Grand Island. Tom Anderson, photography curator of Stuhr and a former colleague at The Omaha World-Herald, deserves a "Good Advice" award as does Bill Brennan of the Grand Island Independent.

It seems we can't do anything without computers these days--one of the few blessings brought to us by the tech age in my opinion--and so it was with this project. Computer people who helped included Joyce Metzger and especially, Duane Fuller of Budget Printing, both of Grand

Island, and Negil McPherson of Omaha. Surprise--
any glitches in this book we can all blame on the
computer.

Two editors who helped more than they'll
ever know were Rosemary Beliveau of Springfield,
Nebraska, and another former newsman colleague,
J. Dennis Burrow, now of Taylors, South Carolina.
The late Hollis Limprecht, World-Herald editor and
author was an early encourager and counselor.
Dave Barber and Harry Dolphin, long-time friends,
gave big assists.

Art sketches for chapter headings were done
by still another talented friend, Marilyn Belschner
of Kearney, Nebraska.

Finally, to those people who provided
personal encouragement and assistance throughout
the 15 months it took to complete this book:
Catherine O'Dowd Gamerl and William M. Arendt,
my son, of Omaha and John Folsom, Robert, Nancy,
Alice, Wes and June, Tim, Shirley and Gayle of
Grand Island.

Table of Contents

v

Chapter	Page

FOREWORD
--from John Easley, a friend

I'm convinced, that as in nature and the seas, there is a time of full tide in the life of man. Such, I would like to think, is how this book came to be. And while it arrives at my personal ebbtide, I would like to think I had something to do with some very fortunate meldings and timings which produced it.

I have known the subject of this book, Fred Bosselman and the Bosselman family, for more years than I care to remember. While we didn't grow up together, we spent more than 25 years in the same neighborhood. Our children grew up in a close group. And, as we all know, when children grow up together so do their parents.

I found that the Bosselmans expected a great deal out of life. They give it a lot. I also know, after four score years of observing and learning on this planet, that those who expect more--and offer more-- will not be disappointed.

My friendship for the author is of shorter span, but nonetheless fulfilling. He came to Grand Island only a few short years ago to assist his wife to return to her mid-Nebraska roots in her final struggle against cancer. My beloved wife of 54 years, Berenice, also became a cancer victim. These two ladies died within weeks of each other, and while they never knew the other person in this world, I'm convinced they're getting along very well together with the Lord right now.

Bill Arendt and I first met in cancer survivors meeting. He had remained active after his wife's death and was the statewide campaign chairman of the term limits petition drive. It didn't take much persuasion for me to join the effort to limit the terms of both state and national politicians. We worked together well. We were part of a winning effort. And I think it was good therapy for both of us.

Close to the end of the term limits campaign I could sense a restlessness in my newfound friend. He had lived in Omaha the previous 40 years. He wanted to return, he confided to me one day, unless he could find a challenge after the term limits campaign. He said he would like to write a book, maybe a company history, if he could find the right subjects. Did I have any suggestons? he asked.

In fact, what you're reading here was my first suggestion.

To me, Fred Bosselman and his family are, in and of themselves, a great lesson for Americans who seem to be searching for value standards. If ever there was a time for us to reach out and learn from family dedication, enthusiasm and just plain love, it is now. Hopefully, this little story will help.

Fred wasn't easy to convince to tell this story. He thought he would be perceived as someone beating his own drums. Both Bill and I told him he needed to realize there was a greater consideration. He could leave a significant contribution to others if and when the story of the Bosselman family were told.

Fred agreed, reluctantly at first. Then, with gathering enthusiasm, came that magic time and tide when all things came together. We can hope we have produced something of value in this book, at this relative moment in time. If that is true, then we are all grateful to have been a part of it.

John H. Easley, M.D.
January, 1994

The Bosselman Family--(standing, left to right) Fred A. Bosselman, Laurie Bosselman, Charlie Bosselman, Fred H. Bosselman, Mary Bosselman Sahling, Scott Sahling, Jim Duncan. (Seated, left to right) Andy Bosselman, Krisha Bosselman, Brandi Bosselman, Jan Bosselman, Chuck Bosselman, Maxine Bosselman, Gene Graves, Barbara Bosselman Graves, Cindy Duncan, Tracy Schultz, Troy Schultz. *Photo by Hal Maggiore*

ix

The Fred H. Bosselman Family in America

(German name: Borstelmann)

Carsten 1845-1923
Married (1872)
Mary Koch (Cook) 1841-1925

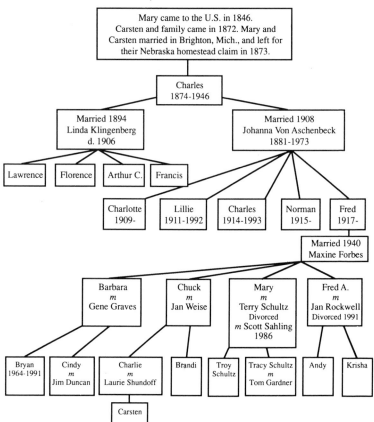

Mary came to the U.S. in 1846.
Carsten and family came in 1872. Mary and
Carsten married in Brighton, Mich., and left for
their Nebraska homestead claim in 1873.

Charles
1874-1946

Married 1894
Linda Klingenberg
d. 1906

Married 1908
Johanna Von Aschenbeck
1881-1973

Lawrence Florence Arthur C. Francis

Charlotte 1909-   Lillie 1911-1992   Charles 1914-1993   Norman 1915-   Fred 1917-

Married 1940
Maxine Forbes

Barbara
m
Gene Graves

Chuck
m
Jan Weise

Mary
m
Terry Schultz
Divorced
m Scott Sahling
1986

Fred A.
m
Jan Rockwell
Divorced 1991

Bryan 1964-1991   Cindy *m* Jim Duncan   Charlie *m* Laurie Shundoff   Brandi   Troy Schultz   Tracy Schultz *m* Tom Gardner   Andy   Krisha

Carsten

Chapter 1

THE LONG WAY UP

Twin headlights froze the center line for a moment. Then there was blackness--total, as the 1941 Ford truck rounded another curve, slowly clawing its way up the steep, twisting two-laner.

Time: 2:45 A.M. Wednesday, August 19, 1942. Place: Highway 6 on the western upslope to Loveland Pass, Colorado Rocky Mountains; 64 miles to Denver.

It was tough going, Fred Bosselman nodded to himself as he shifted his sweaty seat behind the wheel, leaning into the engine as if to help it upwards toward Loveland Pass.

"Can't be much farther," Fred muttered, mostly to himself but also to the young man, Robert Bader, sitting silently beside him in the Ford's cab.

No answer. Fred glanced over. Bader was leaning forward, too, his eyes staring into the night. Scared, Fred thought, just like me.

For two hours and 20 minutes now they had been creeping up this mountain, yes, in the middle of the night. Well, not quite, Fred thought as he glanced at his watch--three o'clock in the morning.

Robert was four or five years younger than Fred--in his early 20's, Fred guessed. He wanted to come along for the ride into this new mountain country. 'Probably his first trip out of Hall County,' Fred mused. He swung the steering wheel to the left and the lights picked up the green-needled trees, more scattered now that they were nearing the top.

This was more than a pleasant truck drive in the mountains, and Robert knew it too. There was no stopping. The Ford was straining, completely geared down. If they didn't make one of these turns, Fred knew, there would be

Spending the rest of the night on the mountain didn't appeal to Fred. He saw no opportunity to turn back.

few, if any, second chances. They would spend the rest of the night on the mountain.

No traffic or help until dawn. Fred shivered. It was getting colder as they climbed. Then he remembered he had done this before, like August a year ago. No big problems then. But it didn't seem quite so slow last year, either.

'Maybe we loaded too heavy,' Fred's thoughts ran back to yesterday when the baseball-sized peaches were being carefully stacked in the rear of the Ford. Man, that was hard work, and that fuzz got all over you, like down the back of your sweat-soaked shirt where you couldn't scratch, and it was always there. It didn't help that Fred had picked up a prickly heat rash during last month's threshing in Nebraska. Barley heads were always toughest to handle in the field. They got into your pores, much worse than wheat, and wheat shocking was bad enough, Fred knew.

He moved his back. 'It still burned and itched,' he decided, even though that shower when they had finished loading had felt good. And it was only five hours since they had left Palisade, Colorado, on their way back to Worms, Nebraska, with a 12,500-pound load of the high country's Alberta Peaches.

Fred's truck was inching up the grade, still in first gear.

'I've got to get to the high side of this next turn,' Fred thought, 'so I can swing a little downhill to get through it. I'll have to use the whole road. Nobody's coming the other way this time of the night anyway--let's hope.'

"Hey, Bobby, what're we goin' to do if this doesn't work?"

There was a grunt from the nearby darkness.

"Maybe we should try backin' down and takin' another run at it," Fred grimaced at the bitter thought of failure. He knew, and Bobby knew, they couldn't back down three-

Fred (left) and his first truck--a 1936 Ford. This is an earlier model of the truck he drove to Colorado. In the driver's seat is Robert Bader and standing, right, are Mel and Robert Meyers, neighbors who from time to time made the peach trip with Fred and Robert but who generally stayed in Colorado for picking.

Above--the J-3 Cub with Fred and his instructor. Right-The 1941 wedding picture of Maxine and Fred. He borrowed the suit from older brother Charles and spent just $60 on the honeymoon.

An early tank delivery truck, similar to the type Fred saw on the home place farm in 1936. This is a 1930 series GMC, one of the first V-8's on the road. *American Truck Historical Society.*

quarters of a mile in coal mine blackness
to find the last level spot where they could   *Passing 11,000*
start over again. No, it was now or never.   *feet and still*
Fred floored the gas pedal.   *climbing: Fred*
     He sensed they were close to the
top. Maybe one more hairpin. Then all of   *remembered*
sudden, Fred remembered, a driver came   *his solo just*
on this wide place in the road and he was   *three weeks*
there. Fred remembered the welcoming   *earlier...*
sign: "Loveland Pass 11,990 feet above sea
level." That's as high as he'd ever been and as high as he
wanted to go.
     Even in an airplane, Fred reminisced. He had soloed
just three weeks ago. Amos Bankson from Polk and Fred had
taken the J-3 Cub up as pilot-instructor and student early
that summer morning, while the birds were still chirping
and the wind was asleep.
     "This is as good a time as any," Amos had said as they
hung in the sky over Nebraska's greenness. "Let me off after
you put it down."
     Minutes later Amos had climbed out. Fred, alone,
pushed in the throttle and took off. He circled the field lazily
and had the Cub lined up perfectly upwind. Over the fence
he cut the throttle and slammed down the tail in a picture-
perfect three-point landing, just as the book said it should be
done.
     "I'll never get much past 10,000 feet in that plane,"
Fred said to himself as the sign Arapaho Basin flashed in the
truck headlights. Maybe one more real groaner turn now, he
hoped, as he shifted his aching back another notch forward.
     He thought of Maxine. How she had hated that
airplane. Particularly when she found out he had spent $12
of their bank balance of $73.55 to get his solo. "Well, it was
done now and you know, I think she actually was proud of me
for that solo," Fred smiled.
     He remembered how he and Maxine put all of their
money into this truck. That happened about a year ago when

*All of their
ready cash
was invested
in this truck.
A year later
Fred and
Maxine had
$693.38 in
the bank.*

they decided there was money to be made in hauling Colorado peaches and Wisconsin dairy calves into the Worms area for resale And it worked.

A year later they had $693.38 in a Mr. and Mrs. Fred H. Bosselman joint savings account in Grand Island's Overland Bank. Payments on the truck were regular, mostly on time.

When Fred and Maxine were married back in September, 1941, less than a year ago, they came to Colorado for their honeymoon. Fred remembered a precious six days in Colorado Springs and Cheyenne, Wyoming. He had sold some hogs and had $60 in cash for the whole week. They both had been careful with the money; they even came back with $3.75.

Trucks had always completely absorbed Fred. Early on, when he was depression-farming with his brothers on the family homestead, he had seen the farm fuel trucks delivering precious gasoline and oil and he had noticed the easy camaraderie among the drivers and farmers. And he still loved to touch the oil-and-dirt-smeared trucks and poke at their engines. One day he had pleaded and then got to drive an International around the farm yard. He was 14 and it had been wonderful!

This was his second year of peaches. Last year he'd made a scouting trip out here to find a peach grower he could deal with. He had to go to Palisade, a good 250 miles past Denver and lot further than he wanted, to find one.

But it was a good deal.

If he ever got this load back to Worms, it should bring a couple hundred dollars clear, after the hauling expenses.

Trucks gave Fred what he wanted--freedom from the confining farm chores he still had to do, but maybe not quite so often if he was hauling stock to Omaha or, for now at least, bringing back peaches from Colorado. Earlier that year he had made a little over two hundred dollars from the sale of Wisconsin calves.

Nothing like a little gamble to get something started, Fred thought. But he and Maxine seemed to be developing steady markets for the calves and the peaches--so why not keep going with a good thing?

~~~

About the time Fred was moving into the early trucking industry, another pioneering Midwesterner saw opportunities for hauling fuel products to the under-served farm market. He was C. J. Hargleroad of Hastings, Nebraska. Hargy, as he was called far and near, started his driving career in December, 1932, when a transport truck sold a load to his station on its way from McPherson, Kansas, a pipeline terminal some hundred miles away.

Hargy felt rail service left a need for farm fuel deliveries. He moved to pick it up.

Hargy knew all the service stations in his area got their fuel for farm resale and delivery via rail tank car. The minimum load was 8,000 gallons, generally offered on a "take-it-or-leave-it" basis of 4,000 gallons of regular and 4,000 of ethyl. Why not, Hargy then reasoned, pick up the loads in smaller quantities more suited to the market needs?

Hargy had a full-time night job at the service station, so his first task was to convince his station owner to stay open at night so he could keep feeding his family, and then he could make daytime runs to the terminal with a truck of his own design. Next, he could convert a Model A Ford truck the station owned into a tank truck.

That was more difficult, Hargy recalled. There was some doubt the Model A could haul 2,000 gallons of gasoline from Kansas to Hastings on a demanding schedule. It took some persuasion time, but the station owner finally

The idea   grudgingly agreed to the conversion,
produced a   particularly if Hargy would do most of it on
partnership.   his own time and at no big extra cost to the
station. Within several months a hybrid
Ford tank truck was born through the expert use of a cutting
torch and welding iron, both of which Hargy knew how to
handle.

Then somebody had to convince service station
operators in the area to use the new system. The Great
Depression, in full throttling grasp at that time, actually was
a plus. Operators liked paying for 2,000 gallons rather than
8,000. Before long, Hargy was in business, now a partner
with his station owner boss.

Maybe the Christmas season helped. In any event,
Hargy hauled his first load of gasoline from McPherson in
January, 1933. He had a couple of customers--and within
hours after he arrived, he had a couple more.

In fact, it was only a few weeks before he was
spending more time in the transport end of the business than
he was in the service station. This created some heavy
problems. A few months more of service station neglect and
Hargy's partner-boss wanted him out.

Hargleroad Transport Service was created from this.
Hargy was bookkeeper, clerk, driver, mechanic and bill
collector. His wife, Dorthea, had a full time job but she even
drove a truck for Hargy from time to time.

Her biggest contribution was the outside job. Hargy
was able to borrow critically-needed money with her salary
as security. In a relatively short time, one truck became two
and two became three.

"I was wearing out trucks," Hargy explained. "And I
had a big crisis after I bought the third truck.

"I had no money, as usual, and the banker wouldn't
lend me any more. I saw this truck that I needed and the guy
who owned it said I could have it if I could make the
payments."

GMC Truck set up this photo of Hargy and his wife, Dorthea, at a
Nebraska Motor Carriers convention when Hargy was president.
Dorthea was primarily a bookkeeper, but she did help Hargy with
the driving when necessary. Below is a 1940's stock trailer rig, a
heavy-duty hauler on graveled Midwest highways in Hargy's days.
American Truck Historical Society.

Truck manufacturers, like auto makers, came and went early in the business. In 1919, Patriot Trucks were big in Lincoln, Neb. The company disappeared a few years later. At right, Harley Shoemaker at his office work bench, one of the busiest spots at the Shoemaker Lincoln truck stop. *Advertisement courtesy Harley Shoemaker, Lincoln.*

"How much?" I asked.

"Sixty-five a month. You can use it until it's paid off. Then we'll talk."

That's the way things were done in the 1930's.

Everybody was paying what they thought they should be paying, so the treasury was empty.

Some years later Hargy ended up as president of the Nebraska Motor Carriers Association. One of his early tasks was to settle and standardize a dues structure. The trucker-members were paying yearly dues only on what they thought they could afford.

Hargy wrote them: "We find that all members are just simply paying 'what they feel like paying' without regard to the size of their operation or the responsibility that they have in maintaining a vital and vigorous trade association concerned about their business and economic interests.

"Therefore, your Directors have adopted a formula affecting all 'for hire' carriers based on one-tenth of 1 percent of your gross annual revenues, multiplied by the percent of Nebraska miles operated.

"For some members that means no increase; for others it means doubling the amount of financial support, and for even a few it multiplies four or five times the amount of your previous financial support.

"Some have asked why? The answer is obvious. We had no fair and equitable system before and we do now. The mere fact that it may have increased some one's support from $100 to $1000 per year means one thing: that member was way off base in comparison to the other members of the Association."

Hargy went on to explain there would be no deals or special allowances in the dues structure. The majority of the board of directors could change the formula, he said, but that was the only way.

And his action helped establish the Motor Carriers at

a time when many people believed truckers were gypsies--
and in some cases, they were right. Truckers lived on the
road, sleeping at odd hours wherever they could. Truck stops
were unheard of then, and there was little or no public
concern about change. The often-dirty jockeys who handled
the big rigs always seemed to threaten everything else on
the road.

Trucks haul five times more than railroads; 18 times more than air.

It has been a long road from those early days to today's trucking industry. This self-regulated freight system now collects 76 percent of the total hauling revenue, that number still growing from the 72.9 percent total handle in the 1980's. By way of comparison, that's five times more than the railroads gross and 18 times greater than air freight revenues.

Deregulated in the 1980's, the trucking industry's
growth has mushroomed, mostly from a new "let's-make-a-
deal" motivation by both shippers and truckers. Competition,
at times cut-throat, helped in that overall growth.

One big factor has been the cost control benefits of
smaller inventories, made possible by more flexible and
timely truck deliveries. This includes the "just in time
inventory" believers. Less than truckload (LTL) carriers are
important parts of this scene and have scored impressive
gains.

Back haul deals, made mostly through load booking
companies, are powering the finances of another industry
segment, the truckload common and specialized carriers.
And this includes a growing number of independent operators.
Private carriers, those trucks owned and operated by large
companies with their fleets dedicated to haul their own
goods, have grown the fastest of all.

All this service industry springs from roots dating
back to the 1890's, when Germany's Gottlieb Daimler
successfully built the world's first gasoline-powered truck.

In this same year, 1896, a small gasoline-powered vehicle which could be called a truck by someone standing far away (as was the practice in those days when no one trusted noisy combustion engines) was developed by the Winton Company of Cleveland.

A runner waving a red flag to warn pedestrians preceded a 20 mph speeder in 1855.

Pre-dating this, however, was the steam-driven wagon, first used in 1769. A French artillery captain, Nicholas-Joseph Cugnot, used it to pull a cannon. It moved at 2.3 miles per hour but because of limited boiler capacity, it could only run 12 to 15 minutes at one time. Poor steering resulted in a final crash.

The steam carriage made its first appearance in America in 1855. New Yorker Richard Dudgeon raced 20 miles per hour down East Broadway and so irritated the city fathers that he was confined to certain streets in Manhattan for the future, and was required to have a runner with a waving red flag precede his vehicle.

Early gasoline-drive truck manufacturers in America included the White and Mack truck companies. International Harvester's first truck was built in 1907. The GMC nameplate started in 1912.

In 1916, GMC set out to cross the continent in a ton and a half truck. It took 31 days of road time and 68 days of elapsed total time to complete the trip. Significantly, there were no mechanical breakdowns--at least none reported by GMC.

It took two wars, however, to really open up America to the potential of trucks. That plus the nationwide construction of the interstate highway system of the 1950's and '60's.

During World War I the Beam Fletcher Company of New York began running 22 trucks a day between that most obvious of transportation connections, New York and

Philadelphia. Later that same year, another company started
regular service between Detroit and Toledo. From there, the
transport system in this country began to change.

The beginnings of any endeavor are fascinating only
if they can be related to individuals and the contributory
impacts on society. So it is with the trucking industry in the
West. Here was a country of comparatively vast distances
between business centers, a new country
developed by and tied to the railroads,
both spiritually and commercially.

It wasn't easy to leave the Mother's Milk of railroading.

It wasn't easy for shippers to leave
the mother lode of railroading--even for
those transportation tasks unsuited for
long and heavy hauls and really not well-
served by rail-oriented interests.

The farmers around Fremont,
Nebraska, for example, had long been
accustomed to delivering their cattle to the South Omaha
stockyards, less than 40 miles away, by rail, even though it
took them the better part of a week between farm loading
and stockyard unloading. Weight and money losses due to
shipping delays hurt. But there was no alternative--until
trucks came along.

Mickey Krupinsky, one pioneer Midwest trucker,
describes his beginnings:

"It was 1922, and I got a job with a Fremont trucking
firm called Union Transfer. The name probably came from
the fact that we hauled only from the Union Pacific Railroad
freight depot to various businesses in town.

"Whenever we got out of town, there was no pavement,
and so we had little or no cross-country hauling.

"Henry Ogram and me--we were Union Transfer,
even though he owned it. We worked seven days a week, at
least 10 hours a day. One evening we were sitting in the
office, and in walks three or four farmers we knew. They
asked us if we could figure some way to get their cattle to

South Omaha faster and in better shape. They said they had whole groups of farmer-shippers in their area who would sign up if we could do the job.

'A profitable back-haul is the goal of all truckers. We stumbled into it.'

Hank and I said we would figure something out, and we did manage to put together a driver- trucker team of half dozen or so units within a couple of months.

"We loaded directly on farms, ran to South Omaha and then back to a different farm to repeat the process." Business was unbelievable. I don't know how many trucks we bought and had operating then. It was fantastic!"

Mickey said that even though they were running mostly on dirt and only sometimes graveled roads, they still made South Omaha within a few hours. On some good days they made three or four trips.

When they caught their breaths some months later, Mickey said, "We realized that if the farmers had trouble getting their goods delivered in Omaha, then the Omaha merchants must have the same troubles getting their goods out to the Fremont area.

"So we stumbled into the ideal of all transportation companies--a profitable back haul," Mickey added.

As roads became paved during the late '20's and 1930's, Union Transfer, now called Union Freightways, moved to Omaha and opened routes to Chicago, Minneapolis, Kansas City, Sioux City and Denver. About that same time another large carrier, Watson Brothers, moved from its start in Nebraska City into Omaha. Watson was later bought out by Yellow Freight Systems of Kansas City, and Union Freightways became part of Pacific Intermountain Express, or PIE, as it was popularly known.

In the 1930's and early '40's, it was difficult to separate labor and management in the trucking industry. Both worked staggering hours, with few complaints. Labor received good hourly and overtime pay. Management and owners started to become rich, mostly by building their entrepreneurships for eventual sale. It was

Hoffa helped trucker management in an hour of need.

a scene from the American dream where common sacrifice, mutual enemies and a booming business bought and brought a team spirit.

No wonder Young Fred Bosselman wanted to get off the farm to join these wonderful knights of the road!

What Fred didn't know, of course, was anything of the struggle it took to get the trucking industry started.

In the early 1940's truckers, both management and the teamsters unions, were being pounded by the ton-mile tax threat in many state legislatures. In its various forms, this use tax supplied revenues from trucking firms based on loads hauled for so many miles. To many, this seemed a fair way to tax and pay for highways.

After all, the railroads pointed out, we had to pay for our roadbeds ourselves (not entirely true because of the huge land grant program offered by the Federal government during the rails' push west).

The truckers argued the ton mile tax would result in strangulation of their infant alternate transportation system and create a hodgepodge of state laws which would defeat any efforts to build a nationwide trucking system.

Mickey Krupinsky remembered an episode with Jimmy Hoffa, then the teamsters' leader in Chicago.

"We had a railroad guy pushing for ton-mile in the Nebraska Legislature and we were trying to raise money to get out our side of the story. Our people were giving up. Nothing was coming in. It was hard times. We were beat.

"In desperation I called Hoffa's office--and this is something management never did, was talk to that bastard except when you had to over the bargaining table--and we talked an hour and a half. I felt like a kid in a schoolroom

For Fastest Daily Service to

East Coast Points

Through Reliable Connecting Lines at Chicago for Non-Stop
Operation to New York and Other Eastern Points,
Fourth Morning Deliveries

SHIP BY

Union Freightways

Phone HA-6333

General Office: 720 Leavenworth Street, Omaha, Nebraska
H. OGRAM, President   M. KRUPINSKY, Vice President

Terminals Maintained at

CHICAGO	MINNEAPOLIS	DENVER	PEORIA
LINCOLN	SCOTTSBLUFF	FT. DODGE	SIOUX CITY
GRAND ISLAND	NORFOLK	FREMONT	

This Union Freightways ad appeared in one of the early editions of
the Nebraska Motor Carriers magazine during World War II days.
The truck line grew tremendously in the 1940's and continued its
expansion , mostly through acquisitions, until it was purchased itself
by Pacific Intermountain Express (PIE)

The Petroleum Transporter Magazine carried this picture in its August., 1937 issue, saying petroleum carriers operating through Kansas pay a half mill per ton mile to use this type of highway. The ton mile tax dispute continued for years in bitter terms. Most states today require truckers to pay a version of the ton mile tax.

answering questions.

"That afternoon I took a call from Council Bluffs across the river in Iowa and the voice said to come to the Chieftain Hotel, Room 207--I'll never forget that number.

"I walk in and the guy, who I never saw before or ever again, started asking me questions about the Nebraska situation. We talk a half hour. Then he points to a suitcase in the corner of the room and says, 'Take that with you and get out of here.'

"I open the suitcase back in my office and it's filled with money, cash--$50, $20 and hundred dollar bills."

Krupinsky said he called an emergency meeting with the largest truckers in the state. They decided to hire a public relations firm and throw a large free-to-the-public meeting in Omaha's auditorium to help get out their message.

"We even got Sammy Davis and Mickey Rooney to help us draw a crowd," Mickey recalled.

There was more than $30,000 in the suitcase. It was all spent. The ton-mile tax proposal was defeated. Nebraska truckers never heard from Jimmy Hoffa again except over the bargaining table.

~~~

"I'm pushin', Fred."

The first words spoken by Robert in what seemed like hours startled Fred as he gripped the wheel and leaned forward. Maybe one more turn now. Then there's that straight piece of road just before the top. The Ford was still crawling upwards, but at a slowing pace. Robert must have noticed. 'He's trying to help,' Fred thought.

Fred inched the wheel to the right as the Ford entered the hairpin.

Take the high side of the curve, then inside and down.

"I'm takin' it out as far as I can, Bobby," Fred said. "We're going to use the whole road on this one."

A few feet before the top of the curve, Fred turned

Cigarette sparks on rear tarpaulin give a scare, but fire isn't the problem.

sharply left and the truck accelerated into the low part of the turn.

'It's working,' Fred figured as he straightened the wheel to keep the Ford on the inside of the turn. "Looks like a flat place ahead. We might make this in one try. Can't stop," he frowned, speaking to no one.

Fred was thinking he'd like to have a cigarette about now. He figured they must be getting close. "We'll stop at the top and check the tarp."

In order to cool the peaches, they had taken off the canvas tarpaulin covering them at the last stop on the way up, about an hour ago. It was on a downhill grade. Fred and Robert Bader had their last cigarette and last relaxing moment then.

No, that's not quite true, Fred realized. Robert had one since and when he threw it out sparks caught on the folded tarp just behind the cab. Fred made Robert hang out the door on his side while they were still moving up to see if there was a fire. Luck was with them then, too. Nothing had happened.

The Ford gained speed through the flat place after the curve, and Fred felt within himself that they had done it-- made it up that mountain.

Suddenly, as they rounded a gentle curve, there was the sign, Loveland Pass--Elev. ll,990 Ft.

They pulled into the observation parking space and Fred killed the engine. The upside was done. He let out a big breath. It seemed he had been holding that one for the last half hour. Almost in slow-motion, Fred opened his door and put his feet gratefully on the gravel. They had made it!

"And now," Fred intoned, "It's only downhill from here."

He smiled as he lit that cigarette.

During a 1993 route-revisited trip, Fred stops his Cadillac at Loveland Pass. Highway 6 has been widened and improved since his 1942 experience, but it still remains a narrow, twisting and steep roadway. Most traffic today goes through the Eisenhower tunnel, except for petroleum or hazardous materials carriers who still must use U. S. Highway 6 over the high pass.

This 1941 model Ford straight truck is like the one Fred used (except for the truck body change) on the Colorado and Wisconsin trips. There were few if any load limit regulations in those days, and Fred could double load and pull a "pup" trailer when he wanted to. *American Truck Historical Society.*

Chapter 2

--One of America's first truck stops, circa 1930

'WHAT? NO BRAKES?'

"What would we have done if a car was coming the other way back there?" Robert asked.

The youngster was suddenly standing beside Fred in the dark, reaching into his chest pocket for a cigarette. He had his jacket on. It was cold on Loveland Pass, at the top of a Colorado mountain, even in August.

"I really don't know, Bobby. I suppose we would have missed each other, even if we passed on the wrong sides. For sure, if the other guy was a trucker he'd know we couldn't stop and would have given us room."

Robert, his cigarette lit, was busy unbuttoning his fly to relieve himself. In the darkness, Fred saw him turn away as the noise of the cascading water hit the gravel like a sudden summer cloudburst. All Fred could see was the bright tip of Robert's cigarette as it hung from his lips.

Fred grinned. 'Why did Robert have to use two hands? Relieving himself on top of a mountain must be an important job,' Fred decided.

But he only said, "Better hurry up . We've got better than an hour into Denver and I want to get there by light."

There was a glow from the east, Fred saw, as he turned back to the truck, taking the last draws on his own cigarette. Maybe that's Denver. If not, it's an early sunrise.

The man from Worms was not

Fred knew there was a God, and he thanked Him.

A small light, almost straight down, the way they were headed.

religious, but he knew there was a God and he knew that God was smiling on them right now. He mouthed the words "Thank You" as he gingerly walked around to the front of the Ford.

It was certainly black up here, and now that the truck's headlights were out, you couldn't see three feet in front of you. He felt his way along the Ford's front fender until he came to the thigh-high stone retaining wall guarding a fall off into the void. He carefully peered over.

There was a small light, almost straight down. A pair of headlights, headed this way. "At least someone else in the world is alive," Fred thought as he turned back to the driver's side of the Ford and opened the door.

"All in, Buddy?" Fred reached into his pocket for the Ford's key.

"Yeah. When do we eat?"

"When we get to Denver. Should be another hour or two."

Fred let his cigarette butt fall from his hand to the gravel. Then he remembered. He stepped on the cigarette, grinding it into the marble-sized rocks and loose sand.

"Can't be too careful up here," Fred said. "What did'ya do with yours?"

"It's out. There's nothin' but rocks up here anyhow," Bader replied.

"Not so. Anyway, always make sure you put 'em out. We could fire this whole mountain."

"Good idea. I could use some heat" was the rejoinder.

Fred backed the Ford out and began the downhill run by throwing the gear lever into third and steering the truck down the center line. He didn't care; no one was coming up the other side right now except for that guy way down below.

A 1919 GMC delivery truck with a 4-cylinder engine producing 37 HP @ 1810 RPM and including hard rubber tires. (Below) A World War I ammunition hauler. Trucks really proved their worth for the armed services in both 20th Century wars. *Photos courtesy the American Truck Historical Society.*

The famous World War II 6 X 6, a two and one-half ton truck for all seasons and all purposes. The late General Patton called it "our most important weapon." More than the Sherman Tank, all of the airplanes and all armaments and equipment (with the possible exception of the Jeep, actually a one-quarter ton truck) the 6 x 6 won the war. *American Truck Historical Society.*

Besides, he could see any approaching headlights minutes before they could reach the Ford.

Fred relaxed in his seat, hitting the brakes only before the downslope curves. Everything was going smoothly. He began humming some unrecognizable tune similar to "Harbor Lights," a popular song of the day. And his thoughts drifted back to Pearl Harbor and last December, the first year of the war, when he and Maxine were trying make do on the farm.

Draft Board refused to take Fred because of high blood pressure, so he then worked harder.

They had been married just a couple of months and had settled in the second house on the original Bosselman homestead a mile and a half east of Worms.

'If they had taken me in the draft I probably wouldn't have worked near as hard,' Fred thought to himself. He was turned down twice by his draft board; both times because of high blood pressure.

He didn't argue with members of the board, most of whom he knew personally. They had already taken Norman, his older brother, and the family thought that was enough. There were more than 1,000 acres to be farmed, and Fred's father, Charles, now an invalid, was unable to help.

Besides, Fred smiled, he was a lover, not a fighter. He had married Maxine. That amounted to another deferment.

Maxine, while tiny and eight months' pregnant right now, was a horse for work. With Fred's farming and part-time trucking, and Maxine's handling everything else, the Bosselmans were always busy, but always doing okay.

He didn't think much about it, but when he did try to analyze the war in Europe, Fred knew that the movement of troops and supplies depended more than ever on trucks. He had read about it, too.

Since Pearl Harbor, just six months ago, the Japanese

Some new opportunities could open up; trucks may be part of the answer, Fred thought.

had really moved. Trucks were actually more useful than boats in Asia as they were in Europe, someone had said.

'So, if trucks are important, then maybe I can be important too,' he thought to himself as he stomped on the brakes at the start of a steep downhill hairpin.

Yes, and maybe because of the war, things are getting better in America, even in Nebraska. Some new opportunities could be opening up.

Trucking could be it. In the months since the war started, trucks became scarce. He'd better be prepared to take advantage of the situation.

Emil Schaaf, a salesman for Central Chevrolet of Grand Island, had been trying to sell Fred an L. J.. Mack truck that Fred dearly wanted. But Fred had never done any bargaining with Emil. Maybe, if he could swing a deal for that truck, he could make a full-time living from trucking. Not a bad thought.

He made up his mind to talk to Charles, the oldest of his brothers, when he got back to Worms. Charles would have some ideas on what to do.

Fred eased into the brakes again to slow for a turn. He straightened. The brakes were slowing them most of the time now.

He'd have to go real gentle on them. That was a heavy load back there. If the brakes ever went there'd be no way to stop.

"I'm going to gear down pretty soon," Fred announced to Robert and to the blackness in the cab. Fred had shifted back to fourth, but he wanted to hold off on the gears as long as possible. Downshifting was hard on the transmission.

"What time is it?" Robert asked.

"You want to stop for breakfast anywhere around here?" Fred gestured to the blackness outside the truck's cab.

"No. We should be in Denver by light, shouldn't we?" Robert was still putting his growling and eager-for food stomach as first priority.

Fred nodded, concentrating on the road and holding pressure on the foot brake.

"We've got Georgetown and then Clear Creek takes us right into Golden. We'll stop there for eats. I'll get us through Denver. Then you can drive."

For just a moment, Fred had forgotten why he had brought young Bader along. When he left Worms two mornings ago, he had five neighbors with him in the truck: Norma and Robert Meyer, Robert's cousin Melvin, and Melvin's sister Rosella, and, of course, Robert Bader. Bader, who was his nephew, actually drove a truck for Fred part-time.

The two couples had come along to pick peaches and stay in Colorado for a few weeks. They had helped Robert and Fred stack the peaches in the truck and then had hired out to the orchard and warehouse for picking and sorting jobs. They would find their own way home next week.

Only the top layer of peaches became bruised. Peculiar.

Robert would drive in relief of Fred on the easier highway stretches. The younger man had driven most of the way out. It was a quick trip. They had left Worms early Monday morning to drive all the way to Western Colorado, to arrive about nine that evening. The peaches had been picked and loaded the next day. The trip back home began that night as soon as the last fuzzy layer was in place.

Funny how only that top layer in the truck becomes bruised, Fred mused. You'd think with all the weight on them, the lower levels of the stacked peaches would be more likely to show wear and tear; but no, it was only the top layer

100 bucks clear made the Colorado trip profitable. But this was Fred's last in 1942.

that Maxine had to cook into preserves. Fred supposed bouncing peaches made good jam.

By the end of the week all 250 bushels would be gone, Fred knew. He and Maxine already had promised close to 150 bushels to friends and neighbors. At a buck, seventy-five a bushel that would bring better than $250, considerably more than Fred had paid the Colorado orchard for the entire load. Then there was another 100 bushels to sell in Nebraska. Most of these would go to the Farmers Union Store in Worms. Louie Heusinger, the manager, had promised Maxine he would sell them without any trouble if he could buy them for around $1.30 per bushel.

'That should bring us another hundred bucks this week,' Fred calculated. A profitable trip.

And this is probably the last trip he'd make out here, certainly for this year, he realized.

Gasoline is going to get tougher to come by. Rationing was already in place, but not for farmers. Fred didn't trust the bureaucrats in Washington. Now they had a war to use as an excuse to get more control.

Trucking could be good in the farm country if the war lasted, and at the rate the Japanese and Germans were going, it could last a long time. Fred had no doubt who would win eventually.

America was gearing up. He read only last week that truck production for the Army was to be doubled this year.

'That's going to mean a lot of trucks on the roads here, too, particularly after the war,' Fred reasoned. He could see the trucks coming and he wanted to be in the front of the parade.

But right now he was coming down a dark mountain road which seemed to be getting steeper.

For the first couple of miles downhill, Fred used his brakes sparingly. Third gear, when he needed it, held back the Ford well. When the grade slacked off Fred shifted back into fourth gear, just to take some of the strain off the engine.

Tough roads and tough loads were the the trials of Fred. He knew he was a good driver.

Now he was on the brakes constantly. He could hear the pads whine and he knew they were getting hot.

"We probably should stop and let these babies cool a bit," Fred said to Robert.

"Let's keep going if we can," Robert replied. Another hour or two on this mountain wasn't going to help his growling stomach.

'Maybe it gets better,' Fred thought to himself as he leaned into another downhill turn hearing, for the first time, his squealing tires. Too fast. He'd have to slow her down more next time. More brakes--now!

Fred realized he was a good driver. He could handle tough roads and tough loads. His runs into Omaha with live cattle were always difficult. A much longer haul--from Madison, Wisconsin, to Worms--with dairy calves was even worse.

Those little critters were jammed into Fred's 14-foot truck and pup trailer, and were delivered, hopefully in good health, to the growing dairy herds of Hall and Merrick Counties in Nebraska.

Fred often used a two-deck trailer and tractor. He brought back close to 100 calves a trip. Those were hairy drives, he remembered. The weather was often rainy and the wind fierce, even though he tried to make the trips in good spring and early summer weather. The calves bawled all the way. And although Fred had his rig fired up to close to

People, like institutions, should be allowed to fail, Fred found out in an Iowa truck stop.

maximum speed, some of the calves arrived in shaky shape after 12 hours in a jumpy trailer.

Before unloading the calves in Nebraska, Fred broke an egg in their mouths and forced it down by tickling their throats. This seemed to calm them and restore a little life for the upcoming sale.

Fred bought the calves for around $15 apiece. He tried to make $10 a head, but some of the calves wouldn't sell for more than $20. Many of those Wisconsin trips were not big moneymakers.

He did learn something, however. The first was that you could be a real hero if you could supply something the neighborhood--or community--needed.

The second lesson was that there were lots of failures out there. People who didn't care, or take time to know any better, should be allowed to fail, he had come to realize.

And he found failures. One was a so-called truck stop in Cedar Rapids, Iowa, where he had pulled in a couple of months ago on one of his Wisconsin trips, weary from 10 hours of driving on narrow Iowa roads, plus another three on Nebraska gravel.

It was a little after midnight. He was directed to a bunk house after he had a sandwich. He wanted to catch just a few hours sleep before continuing into Wisconsin.

There were probably 30 men, all very obviously asleep, in that bunkhouse. The noise was deafening.

Fred thought then and there that if he ever had anything to do with truck stops, he would not put the drivers in a dormitory and he would provide decent meals and services.

Echoes of snores followed Fred out to his truck cab, where he had spent the rest of the night in a tossing, uncomfortable sleep.

The road in front of Fred was unwinding now in what looked to be a gentle downslope.

They were going down a mountain at 45 mph and with no brakes.

Whenever he touched the brakes he removed his foot just as rapidly. He wanted to slow the truck in soft touches and with minimum brake wear. Highway 6 was straight here, and every once in a while there were slight upgrades where Fred could relax his vigil in trying to guess how steep a downhill lay in front of him.

"Georgetown, seven miles," Robert read the roadside sign.

Fred hit the brakes. They had been gaining speed in a sudden, unexpected plunge.

"I hope we don't make it in the next three minutes," he responded. "This is gettin' a little hairy, so hang on."

The speedometer in the Ford never was very accurate, Fred remembered, so it was almost an afterthought that he glanced at it: 45 miles per hour. Not bad, considering he'd been sparing on the brakes.

Then they hit another steep downgrade with a curve. Fred jumped on the brakes again. They slowed to 50. He'd better get back into third gear soon, he realized.

The road leveled as they came into and out of the wider lanes past Georgetown, going just about as fast as anyone had ever run it, especially in the dark.

Fred remembered the corner bar in Georgetown, probably built during the Colorado gold rush around the turn of the century. On a more leisurely trip, he had stopped there once and enjoyed himself.

Fred, at times, liked his booze. A shot and beer would go well right now, in the Georgetown bar. Better if Maxine was along, and they could spend a few hours.

The Ford lumbered past the Highway 40 turnoff to Fraser and a new ski resort called Winter Park. Idaho Springs next.

Still, there was no traffic. They had passed the up-bound car Fred saw earlier at least 15 minutes ago. Nothing on the road ahead but blackness. The highway was good, better than over the pass, but you still had to guess what lay ahead and how steep it was.

Yet he enjoyed challenges like this, Fred admitted to himself.

Trucking could be fun, but 'what will it do to my family?' Fred asked.

"You ever thought about bein' a truck driver, Robert?" he asked his companion.

"Yeah. I think I'd like it, but I don't know who would take care of my folks."

Robert and his brother, Donald Bader, were part of a close-knit family, Fred knew. They often drove for Fred, but just as often declined.

"You wouldn't be home very much, that's for sure," Robert added.

The road was winding now, with sheer rock walls close to each side. Clear Creek country. They were gaining speed. More brakes.

'Speedometer's the same. I wonder if it's working,' Fred thought. 'No, it just seems like we're going faster because we're closer to the cliff walls,' he decided.' Keep on the brakes.'

'You know,' Fred speculated, 'Robert's probably right. Truck driving is fun, but what will it do to my family?

'I don't see being away from home weeks in a row, and that's probably what it would take to go big-time. Right now would be especially bad. With Maxine only a few weeks away from delivering their first born, she needs all the help she can get.'

Fred snickered to himself. 'Maxine wouldn't call me much help.'

He'd never learned to pick up behind himself because he and his brothers always had the women in the house for that--and cooking. The boys' job was to farm and they didn't want to mess with anything else.

Pro drivers never got 'behind the curve' where they were not in control if they could help it.

'Well, I can learn,' Fred promised to himself as he wheeled the Ford around another curve. 'Thank God these curves are gentle and not like the hairpins up above. Maybe, just maybe, I could do something in the service station business,' Fred theorized. 'It would take money. But I might be able borrow it, because my credit's good, I know.'

The road ahead was widening now as they penetrated the Front Range. There was a long downslope ahead, but he didn't know when it began nor exactly how long it ran. He knew he'd have to have plenty of brakes for this one and he'd have to gear down as soon as he felt he was in it.

The problem was that these downgrades were deceptive, especially in the middle of the night. A person never knew for sure if or when he was in serious trouble and in a condition professional drivers and pilots called "behind the curve." That meant the situation was handling the driver, not the driver handling it.

Fred realized it could happen to the best. He was sure Robert didn't, so he didn't say anything.

He began applying heavier pressure on the brakes. The pedal felt warm. Not much slowing.

Fred looked out and behind to his left rear wheel. A few sparks were flying. The brakes were over-heating.

"Robert, check on the right rear." Fred tried to keep

his voice calm.

"It's okay. Wait. You've got some sparks."

Fred cut in: "I'm going into the rear axle."

He threw the rear axle shift lever forward and the Ford's engine became a roar as the downshift took hold. The truck slowed.

Fred thought quickly. Now is decision time. But first things first. He turned to look at Robert.

"Robert, we're losing brakes and we're goin' down a long hill. I can get this baby down to 25 if you want to jump. Now's the time to get out."

Robert hesitated, then raised his eyes to Fred's.

"I'll stay if you're stayin'. How about both of us ditching the truck? We can stop her real sudden-like."

Fred's reaction was immediate. Never give up if you have a chance. Those were his father's words. And there were other reasons. This was a near-new truck. Insurance he couldn't afford, and he couldn't afford to wreck her.

"No." he decided.

'If Robert has that much confidence, then I do too,' Fred's mind was racing as he thought of what lay ahead.

"Okay let's take her down. Get on the emergency, but don't use it 'til I tell you.

"We probably have another five miles and it's all going to be downhill." A pause, then jaws tightening, Fred said: "It should be a real ride."

Chapter 3

DOWNHILL IS ALWAYS FASTER

He tried to see past the headlights, into the blackness. No luck. The Colorado highway people had marked their roadways well, however. White paint on the pavement edges glistened as it slid by the truck.

It's like a race, only the winner won't be able to stop.

'So far, so good,' Fred thought, as he relaxed his muscled grip on the frigid steering wheel. "If I can just keep this baby under 80, we may be OK. The road's fairly straight.

'This will be like a race. Only the winner won't be able to stop to hear the cheers.'

Fred's mind went back to another race, nearly 40 years ago. The Omaha relatives of his mother had told him about the memorable day in truck history, May 20, 1903, in New York City.

The trucking industry was only a few years old at that time, the product of some enterprising Americans who tried hooking a wagon to the back of the new "horseless buggies" just then making an appearance.

Henry Ford had just built his first automobile in 1893 and it took a decade for him and others to bring their new machines to market.

The Automobile Club of America at 58th Street and Fifth Avenue was to be the starting and finishing point for a non-stop speed run through New York. Eleven vehicles were entered, all but one powered by steam.

The winner, Fred remembered, was the gasoline driven truck, a 16-horsepower Knox city delivery vehicle. It

A 1903 race in New York marked the beginnings of today's trucking industry. The first trucks were steam powered.

carried 12,250 pounds of pig iron over the 40-mile course in 3.5 hours. The Knox also won the following day's 100-stop contest. High heat caused breakdowns by the steamers, Fred's in-laws pointed out somewhat gleefully because they had been in the petroleum business at that time.

That was the birth of the trucking industry. Within five years of that race, 4,000 trucks were on the nation's highways--mostly on the East Coast. By the start of World War I, the figure had grown to 300,000 and at the end of that war there were more than one million trucks working in the U. S.

Fred shook his head. He didn't want to think about races or trucks--or anything other than getting down this mountain in one piece, with his load intact.

Light touches on the brakes seemed to slow the truck a little. How long that would work, he had no idea.. At least until the brakes got too hot to hold.

When the brakes did quit, he'd have to depend on lower gears and the emergency brake.

He couldn't help but think of Maxine. He remembered their wedding in the Zion Lutheran Church at Worms. Brother Charles was the best man and Maxine had one of her high school chums as an attendant. What was her name? Fred couldn't remember.

He did remember buying Maxine the ring. He didn't go to the jeweler in Grand Island, Myers, who knew his family. Instead, he went to Michael's Jewelry, down the street and up a half block, and paid $50 for a diamond. He didn't want his friends to know he was planning to marry the "city slicker," as his farm buddies called Maxine.

Fred had met Maxine about a year earlier, at a dance

The York , Nebraska Gamble Store ("We have everything") circa 1940. That's Dwight Forbes, the father, waiting for customers. He didn't have to wait long for Fred when Maxine was being courted. (Below) The Glovera Ballroom in Grand Island, where it all began. *Glovera photo courtesy Bailey Studios in Grand Island.*

This is the home Fred and Maxine came home to after their honeymoon. One bedroom, a living or "sitting" room and a kitchen downstairs was all that was needed. The hired hands slept in the unheated upstairs during winters.

in Grand Island. Fred, a large man at well over six feet, was immediately taken by the petite Maxine. She lived in Central City, Nebraska, about 30 miles to the east. Fred had talked one of his dance hall cronies who had known her brother into arranging a double date, really just a meeting at the Glovera Ballroom. Fred had taken her home that night. Maxine's father, Dwight Forbes, ran the Gamble store in Central City and Maxine worked there, helping him. During the year of courtship, Fred visited the store regularly. He probably became our best customer, Mr. Forbes had recalled at the time.

Fred was one of Maxine's father's best customers. He bought nails every week just to see Maxine.

Maxine really began to think seriously about Fred when he began coming into the store several times a week to buy nails.

"The usual?" she would ask him.

"Yes."

"That will be 10 cents."

Fred, never a big spender, always managed to have some money in his pocket, even in those early years when no one had much cash. He learned that lesson when his sisters and their friends had taken him along to one of his first dances, probably back in 1936. He had no money on him. He had to sneak along the crowd edges to find someone, anyone, he knew in order to borrow something. He finally found a friend--was it Otto Frauen?--who loaned him 25 cents. The buddy was waiting to collect from him the next morning outside of church. And that had been embarrassing.

In those days the Glovera male crowd tested its manhood by buying swallows of drinks. For 30 cents the guys could take a mouthful of peach brandy right from the bottle and chase it with a half-glass of Mogen David wine.

*Fred bought
200 acres
from his
Dad,
married
Maxine
and began
farming.*

Once Fred met Maxine, he knew what he wanted. He was in his early 20's. He could make a living farming. It was time to start a family. Maxine, 19 at the time and just out of high school, had agreed to join him on the farm, and Fred had made arrangements to buy 200 acres and a farmstead from his father. Maxine and Fred would live right on the home place section, about three-quarters of a mile from the home place near Worms.

Right after their Colorado honeymoon, they had moved into an older home already on the place. There he and Maxine began working their 12-hour days, farming and trucking.

During haying season, Maxine perched herself near the unspooling wire on the front end of the baler machine and tied the hay into bales. She also saw that things went smoothly.

She continually was in the field with Fred. Even when he was threshing for neighbors, she would bring sandwiches and some cool lemonade out to where he and the crew were working.

Back in 1936, Fred, along with Charles and Norman, his two brothers, got their first and only boost from the Bosselman family. Each son received $300 cash and a team of horses, plus harnesses, from their father, Charles.

It was understood, but never stated, that they would use their money to get started on farms of their own. All three boys did exactly that, buying back pieces of land from their father at appraised prices, "plus a little bit," Fred explained.

In the mid-thirties, the three boys decided to buy a threshing machine, something of a "used wreck" Charles had called it. They rebuilt it themselves and began offering their services, including machine, to neighbors.

That move eventually brought enough money to Fred--an extra $300 to $400 a year--so that he felt he could afford a wife and family.

But first, he had to have a truck. There was a used 1936 Ford 13-footer down at the International Harvester dealer. It seemed to be in good shape. Fred bought it in April, 1940, for $950, and when the new 1941 Fords came out just five months later, he felt he could afford a new one, the hauling business was so good. The new truck, the one Fred was driving down this steep Colorado road, had dual rear wheels, a 14-foot capacity box, a two-speed rear axle and a four-speed main transmission. It was a good truck and Fred was proud of it.

Fred didn't really blame the truck for running out of brake power. If he could just stop and cool them, the brakes would be fine. But it was too late to stop now.

If they could stop to cool the brakes, all would be OK. But it's too late now.

Fred could feel the peaches heavy on his backside, as the Ford gained speed. He glanced over at his companion. Robert's face was chiseled in the darkness, intent on the road ahead.

"You ready with that brake?"

"Yeah. You want it now?"

"No. Not yet. There's a little upgrade along here someplace. It should slow us a bit."

What Fred didn't say, but knew, is that the upgrade was really just a flatter area where the drop wasn't as steep. He figured there was no use in giving the boy the shakes, too.

Still no traffic, and it was approaching five in the morning.

Fred mouthed a silent prayer that nobody was ahead of him on this road, and that there was no oncoming traffic.

They passed the pickup doing 60 and hoping no one was coming from the other direction.

Then he saw it. A red tail light about a half-mile ahead.

"We'll be on him in a few minutes," Fred said, as he looked at the Ford's speedometer: 60 and holding steady.

"We may have to use the emergency. Be ready."

The rolling truck was gaining on the tail lights. Fred saw it was a light pickup type of vehicle. Probably some farmer going to town early.

Still nothing coming towards them. 'Maybe we'll get by this one,' Fred thought, as he edged the Ford over into the left lane.

In a matter of a hasty breath's time they swooped by the pickup, and Fred steered right again.

"I bet he thought we were in a hurry," Robert said, as they moved quickly out of range of the passed vehicle's headlights.

"We are," Fred replied. "Give me a little emergency. Just a touch, now."

More lights ahead. Oncoming traffic. 'That's not so good,' Fred thought. 'The more cars on this road right now the less our chances of getting through.'

Robert pulled on the emergency and there was an immediate slowing of the truck.

Fred quickly shoved the main gear lever ahead to third and the two men stiffened as the gear's whine consumed the cab. The truck slowed.

"I hope we don't lose it now," Fred said. The first of the two cars approaching them zipped by, the second just a few ticks later.

Fred had noticed the Lookout Mountain turnoff sign a few miles back. They were probably only a few miles from level ground right now, but they were gaining speed all the time, running on a steady downgrade.

"It's not as steep as before, but that's when we had brakes," Fred shouted over the roar in the truck's cab.

"The gears are helping, if we don't rip out the transmission," Robert muttered.

Fred could see more lights ahead, and there was a brightening of the horizon. 'Dawn,' he thought. 'A good time to be racing through Denver streets. Certainly better than eight o'clock, anyway.'

'If he had to pick a time to race through Denver, dawn was probably not too bad,' Fred thought.

The truck's front tires were banging the pavement in a crescendo of sound. Through the open driver's side window their thumping noise became a constant roar.

Fred's thoughts went to tires and the Eagle balloons he had put on this truck just a month ago. They were certainly better than what he had on the farm just a few years back.

Fred remembered when he and his two brothers took over farming from their ailing father. Within weeks, they lost six horses from an equine virus that swept through the area.

A new team of horses was worth about $400 in those days, and that had meant a replacement investment of better than $1,000, probably $1,200. The boys had decided to buy a used tractor to replace the horses, particularly after they talked to their half-brother Art who had been farming on his own for the last eight years and who always was considered a bit ahead of his time. Art was a tractor man.

So they bought the Deere tractor. It had rubber tires. Art had said they would work, but the boys would feel more secure if they had a pair of steel-lugged wheels, too. They

Neighbors told the boys they couldn't raise anything but dust with their new rubber-tired tractor.

then made a deal for the extra wheels, a cultivator and power mower, plus the tractor, for $1,165 cash.

That much money brought them to the bank, but there was no problem because Charles Bosselman, their father, owned 1,041 acres of prime crop land at that time, and the banker was happy to take payments on the equipment if he held a note against the land.

Fred recalled the brothers going to a Farmers Union meeting one night shortly after they bought the tractor.

"You boys are going to find out that your new rubber-tired tractor will just compact the ground and you'll never raise anything," Albert Lauthauser, a neighbor, had said.

Norman had replied, "Well, if we can't do anything else, we'll raise some dust."

The Deere and their new equipment did much better than anyone in Worms suspected. Within a year or two the boys were working the farm well, with their father's counsel and help from neighbors and Brother Art, they were producing record crops of hay, oats and corn. Even the cattle business was good.

Rains came a little more often in the late 1930's and farm prices tended higher. The threshing machine turned into a good investment. Everybody was busy, but everybody was making some money.

Older brother Charles, like their father Charles, was not bossy. The three boys did about everything together and as Norman often said of those days, "You pick on one of us and you take on all three."

Fred managed a faint smile as the Ford plunged down the hill. The gears were shrieking, the foot brakes were useless, giving off sparks in all directions in the pre-dawn

Horsepower was prime power on Midwestern farms even into the 1930's and 40's. Here a field of wheat is cut in preparation for the hand stacking crew following up. It was hot, dirty and sweaty work. Only harvesting barley was worse than wheat in producing skin irritations.

darkness.

'We must give 'em a horrible sight,' he thought to himself as they shot past another car headed up hill.

He remembered his first experience with cars, a Model T owned by his parents. One day the folks went to town in the horse and buggy and, of course, the boys, then in their early teens--and in Fred's case, barely 10--got the Model T out of the garage. They all had driven it around the machine shed, each carefully taking his turn.

Then they had put the car back into the garage, just like it was before. But they had forgotten to wipe out the tire marks around the shed.

Fred remembered his father looking at the rutted dust, and knowing what had happened, but he never said a word to the boys.

When Carsten Bosselman, Fred's grandfather, died in 1923, he left around 1,000 acres of prime land east of Worms to Charles and his three sisters. Charles, who now was called Charles the Old to distinguish himself from his son, Charles the Young, bought the farmland from the three sisters. When Charles the Old took sick in 1930, he owed the bank $44,000. How Fred's mother got them through the 1930's with those kind of loads: debt, drought, depression and sick husband, Fred will always marvel.

Fred's father always had a way of making do, however. He had gone to Grand Island's business school and he used his learning well in advising his fellow farmers in legal matters. This was especially valuable to many of the non-English speaking farm people in Central Nebraska.

Charles the Old also was a carpenter. Before he became ill, he

Fred's Dad could always make do, even though he was sick the last 16 years of his life.

practiced his trade over the region and provided an extra source of income to his growing family.

Fred, only 13 at the time, remembered well his father's sickness. He was kicked by a horse and taken to St. Francis Hospital in Grand Island. The leg wound healed slowly and Charles the Old begged the doctors to let him stay at his sister's place instead of the hospital for his final recovery days.

The doctors gave in to him finally, and just as he was getting back on his feet, he decided to go to a sale at the Fred Peters place. He caught cold and became desperately ill. Back into the hospital he went.

Within a few hours, infection had set in. And within a day the diagnosis was complete. Charles the Old had encephalitis. He was taken home a bed-ridden invalid, unable to feed himself or take care of his toilet.

Charles the Old would make a list every day of things to be done, and the boys would do them.

The following days and weeks became nightmares as the family all pitched in to help. Fred's mother and the two older sisters, Charlotte and Lillie, managed the house and cared for the sick father. Charlotte even made a crude walker for Charles' use the few times a day he could get out of bed.

Charles the Old would make a list every day of what needed to be done. The boys split up the work and, with the exception of the tough job of handling cattle during the worst winter weather, did all of the farming.

Charles the Young was 15, Norman 14 and Fred 13 during those early farm management trial years.

"We got along great because we didn't have time to get into trouble," Norman explained later. "Those early years are like a blur. Fred and I quit school at eighth grade.

Charles was in high school and continued on in that because he had good grades, but even then, he had to quit before he was graduated."

Charlotte became a school teacher with lots of drive and ambition.

Charlotte, four years older than Charles the Young, never stopped in her drive to become a teacher. She had a bright, inquiring mind and the unflinching will to succeed. It took her through high school in Grand Island, two years of college in Kearney and teaching jobs in country schools in Merrick County, all goals reached before she was much older than the kids she was teaching.

"Charlotte always had more ambition than all of us put together," Norman said. "She would take care of Dad, clean the house, leave something in the oven and then go to school. She'd come back and repeat the same bit and then go to bed around midnight, only to start the next day at dawn."

Charlotte was always ahead of her times, too. Esther Van Pelt of Hordville, one of her students, recalled that a black classmate had a death in the family and that everyone hesitated to go to the funeral. Charlotte ignored her superintendent's advice not to become involved. She went to the funeral and established a pattern of care and concern which her students noted and followed in their lives.

Under the constant care of his wife, Lillie, Charlotte and the three boys, Charles the Old began to show slight improvement over the next few years. His mind always worked well. He got around with the help of a walker. He called farm management meetings with his three sons and whoever was working as a hired man at the time. There he'd outline what needed to be done, when and sometimes, how.

Charles, the son, recalls the day he turned 21. "Dad called me in and said: 'I'm going to begin paying you $20 a month for your work around here.' "

*Charles
went
to school,
and he had
ideas on
how to
irrigate
the farm.*

"That's not necessary," Charles replied. "I'm getting food and a room, and that's enough while you're still sick."

"No. The going pay for a man's work on a farm is $20. That's what you're getting, starting today." Charles the Old wouldn't have it otherwise. Charles even kept his place at the family's eating table- -no extra charge.

Charles the Young had just completed a couple of part-time study years at the Grand Island business college his father had attended 40 years earlier.

· He was full of ideas, and he unloaded them rapidly on his younger brothers.

They were going to irrigate the farm, Charles decided. Alfred Wagner, a neighbor, had just put in an irrigation well. He didn't have far to go into the clay soil. The water table east of Worms sometimes was at ground level, seldom more than three or four feet under the surface.

Charles approached his father. He knew he stood a good chance of convincing him to do something new. Charles the Old always was the innovator, the first in the neighborhood to have anything new.

"Dad, we got level fields out south. If we could build an irrigation system, we could double our corn yield. Alfred Wagner just put in a well, and he said he'd help us," was the way Charles approached his father.

There was no doubt. The next week, the well went in, and a 600 gallon per minute pump was installed.

The boys worked steadily for three weeks to get the pump and gravity irrigation system ready. They figured they had no leveling to do since the land already was flat as the pool table they all used to practice on in Palmer.

The magic day came when the water began spewing

Here's a typical Midwestern threshing crew with its steam powered energy. Even during the 1930 depression there were touring neighborhood threshing crews. This is undoubtedly one of them. *Photo courtesy of Stuhr Museum, Grand Island.*

Early on in the dry Midwest--and certainly after the drought of the 1930's--irrigation became an important way of life. Most larger farms had their own pump irrigation systems and many drew water from the gravity irrigation ditches cross-stitching the central and western part of driest Nebraska. *Stuhr Museum photo.*

Charles the father and Johanna, his second wife, were married in Worms in 1908. Linda Klingenberg, Charles' first wife, died in the early 1900's after giving birth to three children. Johanna was also a German immigrant from near Hamburg, and a sister of the Rev. J. Richard Schroeder, the sodhouse preacher who was pastor in Worms at that time. See Chapter 4 for more on the life and times of the Rev. Schroeder.

Carsten Bosselman, the founder of the clan in America, surveys his neatly clipped hedges and evergreens just outside the family place near Worms. Carsten was a great naturalist, planting trees and introducing wildlife to the entire area. (Below) A deer just outside the home place's fencing is caught by the camera in the early morning light of Easter Sunday, 1909.

from the black earth to spread over the corn rows. The boys had built small ditches to guide the irrigation water into the proper corn rows.

But wham! Everything happened too fast, and there was too much water too soon. Forget the ditches. They were washed away. The water roared into the southeast corner of the field and stayed there.

"Looks as though we got to level this field, boys," was Alfred's way of stating the obvious.

The brothers were lucky to get their corn crop in that year. The southeast part of the quarter section never did dry out completely.

They did begin leveling the field that fall. By the following spring everything was in place for another irrigation try. This time it worked! Just as Charles had promised his father.

Bosselman was nearly drought-proof in the dry years of the 1930's.

The Bosselmans were near drought-proof through the mid-1930's because of that irrigation system. It had been expanded yearly to cover all but the hay pastureland.

Wild hay took up almost a third of the 860 acres the Bosselmans were farming then. It produced two natural crops a year, without having to do anything but stack it.

The hay was fed to the 100 head of cattle the Bosselmans kept on feed on the farm. There was a good-sized dairy herd, too, maybe 20 to 30 head.

"We never went much for sheep," Charles the Younger said. "A lot of people did, and they could make it or break it in a hurry with them."

Hay, corn, oats, rye and a little barley gave the Bosselmans plenty to do on the growing farm.

Norman, who describes himself as 'the one true farmer in the family,' explained: "We had a good spread.

Many of the early settlers moved on west when they failed at farming.

Grandfather Carsten picked it out after he found his first choice in land around here was really a wetlands parcel with not deep enough soil. He sold it to a relative and bought the present farm.

"Within a couple of miles north and west of Worms, you run into a hard clay and, in some cases, the beginnings of Nebraska's Sandhills region. So it's critical that you have the right soil. We did."

Many didn't. In the early days of homesteading, and certainly after the better land parcels were claimed, settlers likely tried farming for a year or two and then, broke, moved on--probably to California or other parts west.

Freida Schipmann said her family got part of its land in Central Nebraska simply by being there. A busted family had told her parents, "You can move into our house the way it is now and stay as long as you like. We may or may not be back." They never came back.

~~~~

Fred's thoughts were ranging back to his early days. Maybe that's how everyone did it when they were facing a danger. He had been staring at the road so long his eyesight was blurring. He blinked a dozen times. That was better.

"Bring on the emergency," he shouted to Robert, hoping the young man could hear him over the roar in the cab. "I'm going into the rear axle."

Fred threw the rear axle gear level forward with all of his strength. There was a sudden explosion of noise. The Ford bucked, slowed like she had run into a clothesline, bucked again and again. Fred thought the whole engine was blowing up.

Robert was holding the emergency brake up as far as it would go with both hands, his face highlighted with sweat and effort.

"Not much left," he grunted.

Fred was concentrating on the road ahead. Still no traffic. Lucky. He could pick out the lights of Golden now. There was some traffic down there, he noticed.

The Ford's speed had dropped to less than 40, but the speedometer was inching up again. There were no more options.

There were no more options, Fred knew. Now it was only luck they needed.

Fred didn't think of praying. He did think he needed some help, and he thought to himself, 'If you get me out of this one, Lord, I'll be your Number One guy in church.'

Actually Fred wasn't promising much. He already was a lay leader in the Zion Lutheran Church of Worms.

But it did get him thinking about the church and Maxine. 'We've got to get a new rectory built this year,' Fred thought. 'But why should I be thinking about that when I'm driving for my life down this doggone mountain?'

Fred never thought--or said anything--in terms of four-letter curse words or blasphemies.

'I know. It's because Maxine is eight months pregnant and I gosh-darned better get Uncle Dick Shroeder out here for the baptism. I was supposed to write him last week, and I forgot.

'I'll do it tomorrow. . .If there is a tomorrow.'

The Rev. J. Richard Schroeder was quite a name in Worms. In fact, it was he who had named the town nearly 50 years ago.

He was the original sod-buster preacher who came to Nebraska when there was nothing but Indians, buffalo and miles of unbroken grasslands. A few settlers, maybe a family every 20 or so miles along the Platte River Trail and four or five over the 100-square mile Sandhills.

The Reverend Schroeder was also the brother of his mother, Johanna, Charles the Old's second wife. Charles' first wife, Linda Klingenberg, died in 1906 following childbirth. Charles married Johanna Von Aschenbeck, who had just immigrated from Germany and settled in Omaha, in 1908. Pastor Dick, founder of Zion Lutheran and headquartered in Worms since 1895, had introduced his sister to Charles and encouraged their marriage.

Fred's mind was skipping as fast as the Ford was moving down the mountain right now. He remembered the story Uncle Dick used to tell about his brother who came to America and Omaha around the turn of the century.

One day the brother asked his employer, a family by the name of Neuhaus, if he could use a two-cent stamp to send his German family a letter.

Mr. Neuhaus said yes, that was fine, but the brother would have to deduct that two cents from his weekly wages of 10 cents.

Fred admired German thriftiness. He was forced to watch the pennies himself. But he never got to that point, he admitted.

Robert had released his stranglehold on the emergency brake by now, looking helplessly at Fred. The emergency was useless.

Approaching the first stop light at 60 mph and no way of stopping. It turned green as they roared through.

The foot brakes had long gone, and Fred knew his rig was barreling down the mountain at better than 60 miles an hour, approaching the first stop light with no hope of even slowing down in case there was cross traffic.

Fred leaned on the Ford's horn as they approached the first red light. "Just pray, Robert," he said.

They roared through the intersection. No traffic. Plain luck.

A small truck was stopped at the next light which was also red.

Fred noticed the driver pulled his vehicle to one side as they blasted towards him. 'He must know. Or he's as scared as we are,' Fred thought.

They seemed to be slowing a bit. The light turned green just as the Ford hit the intersection, and Fred saw two cars approaching from the north on the side street. Lucky they were slightly late.

Fred, Robert and peaches went through the next two cross streets without trouble and Fred was finally able to gear down the main transmission to second, then first. This brought the truck to a stop a dozen or so feet from a major intersection with lights and waiting traffic.

Ten minutes to six in the morning, Fred's watch read. He and Robert could see without headlights now as the gray dawn brightened.

The truck finally stopped a few feet from a major intersection and waiting traffic.

Fred spied a 24-hour diner up the street on the right, about two blocks away.

"Let's get some breakfast. I've had about enough of this truck cab. OK?"

Fred didn't have to wait for Robert's answer. He moved the Ford slowly through the green light, glancing to both sides to see several cars and small trucks waiting for the light change.

"Good thing we didn't have to bust through this one," Robert said, motioning to the busy intersection.

"Now you talk real big, Robert. Why are you still holding on to that emergency brake?" Fred smiled.

Robert erupted in laughter. "The way you drive, I had

*They really
made it, but
the brakes
would have
to cool
down in
a hurry.*

to hang onto something. Did we really make it?"

"Yeah. But I may have to clean up my pants in this place," Fred replied as he turned the Ford into the parking lot and inched into a vacant spot. He had to go to first gear to stop the truck.

"Maybe these brakes will cool down so's we can use 'em again," Fred said as he opened the truck cab door and stepped down to the asphalt parking lot. "Never thought I'd be so happy to touch ground."

The pair filed into the restaurant, led by Fred. They sat down, really slumped, in the nearest booth. There were only four other people in the diner and the waitress approached them quickly.

"Coffee, twice. Black." Fred ordered.

The waitress was there with coffee pot in hand, and Fred took a couple of sips before he went to the gents room to wash up.

Fred's shirt stuck to his back and his legs were stiff as he walked to the back of the diner. He remembered Maxine's trouble with shirts, right after they were married.

Fred had mentioned he liked starch in his shirts. Maxine had proceeded to dump the entire starch box into the next wash. When Fred had picked up his laundered shirt, it was like a cardboard box. He had told Maxine she had used too much starch and she cried. Fred had worn the shirt that day, anyway.

Robert and Fred ate well that morning. Eggs, bacon, hash browns, toast and jelly. They took their time. Fred knew that if the brakes refused to work they were going nowhere.

So they chatted on through the hour. Robert went out twice to see if the wheels were still hot, and he reported they were cooling. Fred figured they'd be ready to roll by nine.

That should put them back in Worms by suppertime.

Sure enough. Fred tried and felt some brake pedal resistance by eight-thirty, and he allowed as how he could get them through Denver's traffic if he took it slow and easy.

Another half-hour and Fred turned over the wheel to Robert just past Commerce City, on Denver's north side. Then Fred slept as the peaches headed for home.

Chapter 4

THE BEGINNINGS

When Fred awoke, the hot August sun was riding high. Robert had the window open on the driver's side, as did Fred on his side. That was the only thing saving them from boiling alive.

It still must be morning, Fred decided. The outside air was still fresh.

"Where are we?" he asked.

"Just coming up to Sterling. We should be in Ogallala by dinnertime," was the response.

"Have you checked the tarp?"

"Yeah. It's fine, but I'll bet those peaches are getting hot."

Fred slowly pulled at his belt buckle, loosened it and rolled his body to the right side, away from the sun. Another few minutes of sack time couldn't hurt.

Instead he began looking out the window at the welcome sight of trees along the Platte River waterway. They stood like green soldiers in a world of browned ground and bright blue sky.

Uncle Dick, the Cowboy Preacher, was a force in the West, a legend by the time he named Worms.

Must have been like this 50 years ago when Uncle Dick was known throughout this country as the Cowboy Preacher and this road was little more than a graveled pathway. Nebraska's Panhandle country, north of here, was where the Reverend Schroeder operated.

Stories of Uncle Dick were re-

peated all over the Worms community and the Zion
Lutheran Church. He was a legend by the time he arrived
in Central Nebraska shortly before 1900.

The original Worms was a city in Germany's
southwest Rhine Palatinate country along the Middle
Rhine River, hilly and famous for its wines and religious
history. Martin Luther was excommunicated by the Pope
in the Edict of Worms, dated 1521. An agreement on the
separate powers of church and state was signed in Worms
in 1122 A.D. The city's founding went back 3,000 years
and to the early days of the Roman Empire.

The circuit preacher covered NW Nebraska, the Black Hills and Wyoming, Montana.

J. D. (Dick) Schroeder was born
in 1872 in Westerburg, Germany (the
home province of the Bosselmans).
He came to America in 1887 and began his religious studies later that
year at Concordia Seminary in
Springfield, Illinois.

Following graduation, he became a circuit preacher in Northwest
Nebraska, the Black Hills region of
South Dakota, Wyoming and Montana.

Preacher Dick, his brother Henry and their sister,
Johanna, had settled in the Omaha area earlier. The
family was a constant and relatively close base of support
for the ranging Cowboy Preacher.

His first assignment was at Crawford, Nebraska,
adjoining Fort Robinson in the extreme northwest corner the of state. This was truly cowboy and Indian
country in 1892. A troop of cavalry, all black with white
officers, was quartered at the Fort. Of 120 houses in
Crawford that year, 92 served either brothels, gambling
or saloon interests.

There was plenty for a preacher to do, the young

The Rev. J.D. (Dick) Schroeder, the pioneer sodhouse preacher who traveled and helped bring church services to Western Nebraska around the turn of the century, and his bride. They later took a pastoral assignment in Wisconsin, but returned to Nebraska frequently as the Bosselman family was growing up.

This sodhouse dugout often was a start on a more elaborate, above-ground sodhouse. Here Solomon Butcher, and early photographer, is shown outside his "diggins" on or about 1880. Part of a homesteading family,Butcher quickly concluded that laying sod for a house on the Nebraska prairie for 75 cents a day was the work "of a fool." He took up photography shortly after this experience. *Photo courtesy of The Nebraska State Historical Society*
from John Carter's book, SolomonD. Butcher, University of Nebraska Press.

Sylvester Rawling's sod home in Central Nebraska, complete with cow on the roof. Rawling was a Civil War veteran. (Below) The type of train Reverend Schroeder used for his missionary trips to South Dakota, Wyoming and Montana in the 1890's. *Photos supplied by the Nebraska State Historical Society, from Solomon D. Butcher book.*

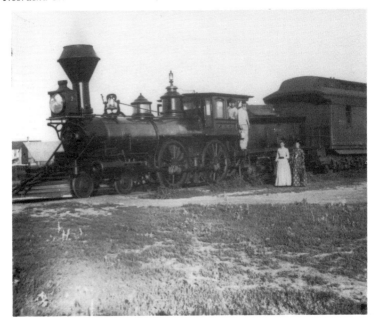

Schroeder decided.

His "missionary" assignment was to locate all German-speaking settlers in this barren land, determine if they were Lutheran and then convince them to establish a church with him as their pastor. He would then visit the church at least once a month.

The preacher founded churches over the area. Often he would set out alone into the wilderness.

Pastor Dick's only lifeline was the railroad. He could ride it all over the four-state area and get to within 20 miles of most of his church members.

When he didn't have money for the railroad, which was often, he would borrow a team and wagon—or just a horse—and set off for days in the wilderness.

Fred remembered reading an account of one of the Cowboy Preacher's first visits. This was his tale, as contained in the <u>Old West Journals of the Rev. J. D. Schroeder,</u> *(copyright, 1989 by Wanda M. Schroeder Oelrich)*:

"I hurried to the Crawford depot, if you could call such a shed that. Finally, after a long wait, the train arrived. Because a single locomotive was unable to pull the train into the hills, a second locomotive was attached. When this was done, we set out.

"After a 70-mile trip, I arrived in Alliance in the pre-dawn hours. Because I knew nothing of the environs, I stayed in the depot until sunrise.

"I wandered into the countryside to find the home of a Mr. Gottlieb, the farmer whose name was provided to me earlier.

"He lived in a soddy like every other farmer. These sod houses were actually very practical and were not costly or hard to build.

"First the prairie was plowed and the stubborn

Interior walls of a sodhouse were 4 feet thick--ideal for winter-summer insulation.

turf raked up into four-foot long pieces. These pieces then were placed upon each other with openings left for doors and windows. Goth gables of the house came to a point, and a beam was laid across them. Then planks were laid, followed by a layer of brush over which more sod pieces were placed.

"The interior walls, which were about four feet thick, were covered with clay and then usually painted with whitewash.

"Such a soddy was very strong and gave refuge to everyone through the many storms on the prairie. It also had the advantage of being warm in the winter and cool in the summer.

"Mr. Gottlieb's house was exceptionally large, with three rooms. One room served as both kitchen and living room, and both the other rooms were bedrooms.

"Again, I was received most cordially. After breakfast, Mr. Gottlieb hooked up his team of horses to a wagon and we set forth to invite all the Lutherans in the area to a church service which would be held the following morning, a Sunday. The service was to be held in a schoolhouse four miles north of Alliance. All the families that we found promised to come. After a long ride with much riding around, we returned home in the evening, two very tired people.

"That night turned out to be most unpleasant. As soon as I got to bed, the bold, ever-present vermin covered me. Finally, I got out of bed and made a place for myself on what might be called a sofa in the room. Sure enough, the bedbugs soon found me there, too. In desperation I went outside and slept on the ground, rolled up in a blanket. It was a cool, September night, and when I awoke the next morning, every bone in my body ached.

Boards served as benches; a large trunk became a desk and the altar was made of sod.

"After breakfast, I quickly went over my sermon, and then we left for the schoolhouse. It turned out to be made of sod and not much better than the sheep stalls of my childhood in Europe except that on one side it had two windows.

"The school benches were nothing but raw boards nailed together. The teacher's desk consisted of a large trunk. Since there was no chair available, my seat turned out to be several pieces of sod piled together.

"Soon wagons and riders arrived from all directions—here, a plain old farm wagon on which the owner with his better-half sat enthroned on the high seat and behind them sat numerous children. There a buckboard, a very indescribable mode of transportation. A great number of the visitors rode spotted ponies."

The Cowboy Preacher continues, "When we realized that no one else was to be arriving, we all stepped into the schoolhouse and the few benches were soon filled. The farmers brought their wagon seats inside and sat on them, while others sat on the window sills. The last ones to enter had to stand.

"My joy over this large gathering was immeasurable. After I put on my robe, I passed out the hymnals which I had brought with me. Most of the people had their own hymn books. Finally I was ready to begin.

"In the name of the Father, the Son and the Holy Ghost,' I said.

"Instantly the room was quiet.

"Let's begin with the hymn, 'Dearest Jesus We Are

Everyone sang loudly, each with his or her own tune or melody. A good time was had by all.

Here,"' I said.

"Immediately there arose a great commotion. Those who had brought their own books looked and looked, and leafed through their hymnals to no avail. Finally one of the ladies found the hymn and shouted to her husband across the room (the men and women sat on opposite sides), 'Jan-Henry, it's on this page here.'

"Jan-Henry looked and looked through his book and could not find it. He asked loudly, 'Lisa, where is it?'

"Lisa had either lost her patience or was embarrassed by her husband, and shrieked back, 'Jan-Henry, you dumbkkopf, open your eyes. It's on the page right there.'

"So it went, back and forth, midst mutterings and grumbling until everyone finally found the song, and peace reigned again.

"I began to sing the hymn. At first, I sang alone. By the end of the second stanza someone joined me until finally, little by little, everyone was singing heartily—each in his own melody.

"The heading over the hymn read 'According to its own melody' which was taken literally by everyone present.

"Following this hymn I gave a prayer and read a scripture lesson. Then I looked for another hymn which would be unknown to them, so that I could sing undisturbed by myself and, hopefully, everyone would get a message.

"In the sermon I told them that I had come to preach the good news of lasting peace and life for all

Some sodhouses could become castles on the Plains. Isadore Haumont built this one in 1884 for $500. It has walls three feet thick, French doors and stood 19 feet at the eaves. *Nebraska State Historical Society.*

This Danish Lutheran church was constructed in 1879 a hundred or more miles east of where Pastor Schroeder preached. The comparisons of what he had and what type of buildings people were used to further east even in the same state, was startling. This church is now on the grounds of the Stuhr Museum in Grand Island. *Photo courtesy Stuhr Museum.*

sinners. They listened attentively and the tears began to flow over some cheeks. They later told me that they were tears of joy that they were at last able to hear the Word of God out there in the West.

'A beautiful service" and they all wanted him back to help them celebrate the Lord.

"After the service I asked them if I should return. As if in one voice they told me to do so. They told me how happy they were that I had come to serve them. I informed them that I could return in four weeks. The men told me that the schoolhouse was inadequate for the church service, and they would ask the Methodists who had a roomy building in town if they could meet in their building.

"This was a promising beginning. The outlook for the founding of a congregation was very good.

"Afterwards, in front of the schoolhouse the people gathered around, shook my hand and thanked me for the sermon.

"An old grandmother said, 'It certainly was a beautiful service. How I thank God that I lived to experience the fact that God's Word would be preached here in our language. Even if the singing didn't go as well as when we were in Germany, it still came from the heart and our dear Heavenly Father surely sees what's in the heart.'

"I overheard a farmer tell Mr. Klein that the 'preacher' could come and stay with them since he lived nearer to town.

"Right away I explained to my host that I would like to go with the man so that I could become better acquainted with him.

"So, off I went with my new friend, Mr. Klein, to his farm. His house, too, was a sodhouse, as were his horse

Somes flies had come to an untimely death in the hot soup. Indeed, they were not raisins.

and cow stalls. Like everywhere else in the new territory there were neither trees nor shrubs.

"Mr. Klein and I sat outside along the wall of his soddy in the hot sun and waited for the Sunday noon meal. Soon his wife called, 'The meal is ready. Come in.'

"As I stepped into the house I noticed that there was only a single room which served as dining, kitchen and bedrooms for the entire family. As I opened the door a large rooster flew into the house and onto a bed, where a hen cackled even as she was laying an egg between the pillows. The rooster jumped behind the hen until the wife energetically and unceremoniously drove them both out of the house with her broom. Finally we sat down to eat.

"After I spoke the table prayer, the housewife said amiably, 'Now dig in.'

"To my great pleasure she had prepared chicken soup with dumplings. My favorite! My appetite was ravenous. When I had filled my bowl, I noticed many little black dots next to the large dumplings.

"At first, I thought that they might be raisins, but it wasn't long before I realized that they were flies which had come to an untimely death in the hot soup.

"The entire house was filled with flies, and sat in every bowl. I fished them out of mine, and ate. It tasted like chicken soup but with a peculiar flavor. I soon discovered why. Due to the lack of wood and coal for fuel, the farmer gathered dry cow chips for his fuel. Everything smelled and tasted of the stuff. But it wasn't long before I grew accustomed to it and didn't even notice it after a while.

"While I was eagerly and busily eating my soup, all at once I felt something moving around under the table at my feet. I thought it was one of the children who might have crawled there.

The family had a pet sow who visited during meals to beg a few favors.

"But suddenly a huge sow stuck her head up from below between me and Mr. Klein who sat next to me.

"I'd love to have seen the look on my face at the appearance of this unexpected guest. The farmer threw out a large dumpling toward which the pig waddled with great pleasure.

"She blinked slyly at me with her little eyes, but when I gave her nothing she wandered over to the other diners and took their tributes.

"Indeed she was the family sow, their pet, which had such a special place in their household.

"Needless to say, I wasn't prepared for this. When the meal was over, to my joy we went outside again. It certainly was beautiful out there in the sun and fresh air.

"Mr. Klein spent the entire afternoon telling me about his trip out west by covered wagon and the beginning of their life on the prairie. Few people can imagine the hardships, obstacles, privations and dangers the pioneers in the west had to battle against.

"Towards evening, Mr. Klein drove me in to town with his team. As I made my farewells to the family, Mrs. Klein said, 'Oh, how wonderful it was today. I'll never forget it.

'It has made me so happy. You can always stay with us even if overnight. I'll make room for you and we'll always have enough to eat.'

"I thanked her for her heartfelt invitation, but in

The preacher never wore his black suit again. His joy was dampened when he thought of what was ahead.

my heart I hoped that I would never have need to accept it.

"Later on though, I often had worse quarters, and sometimes none at all...

"The next morning at about 5 o'clock, I returned to the little town of Crawford and walked the nine miles back home. My joy to be back home again was dampened by the thought of what lay ahead in my chosen calling.

"When I reached the house I proceeded to give myself a thorough scrubbing. When I first came out here, how nice my black suit had looked. Now it was a mess. It became clear to me that I wouldn't be needing it anymore out here. I brushed it, hung it up and never wore it again.

"From then on I wore a practical, durable suit in which no one in a civilized place would expect to see a pastor."

Though his family's beginnings in America were humble, Fred realized, the earlier Bosselmans were anything but.

His grandfather, Carsten, left Oldenburg, near Hamburg, Germany in 1868 with little more than his knowledge of farming, his love of the land and its creatures and a willingness to work. He was 22 years old.

The Dammanns and the Bosselmans came to Michigan together, where they settled in a new Oldenburg farming community. In Germany the family name had been Borstelmann or von Borstelmann, but, as happened to so many immigrants, the name was inadvertently—or on purpose—changed by the time the family arrived in

America.. Too many wars in the Old Country caused too many men to be drafted to serve in armies they didn't want to serve in and hence promoted heavy immigration to America with a name change.

Life was tough, but never so tough the immigrants wanted to return; they seldom complained about things.

It was tough, Carsten later told Fred and his brothers, but never so tough they wanted to return to Germany. In fact, the immigrants felt so fortunate to be in America they seldom complained about any work or any pay. That attitude served them well for many years.

Carsten immediately apprenticed himself to a farmer in Michigan. One of the big jobs for the eager, young German was clearing land for crops. Within a few days the farmer offered Carsten 80 free acres if he would eliminate the trees and stumps on another 160 acres.

Carsten may have been new to the country, but he was no dummy.

Michigan was heavily forested. The trees on that particular section were no more than five or six feet apart.

Carsten figured he'd be an old man by the time he got the area cleared and took his 80 acres payment. And he also knew about the free land the U. S. government was offering in Nebraska, ironically for just settling there and planting trees.

So he and his bride, Mary Koch, Claus Dammann and Carsten's two brothers, John and Claus, joined an immigrant train to Nebraska. Everything they owned, including animals, went into a railroad car, along with two other west-bound neighbor families and whatever

The nearest trees were in the Loup River Valley, about 20 miles away. In winter, they brought the animals inside.

they owned. Crowded it was—for the five days it took them to reach the Grand Island area.

Carsten no sooner settled on a homestead 16 miles northeast of Grand Island than he went to work for the railroad in Grand Island.

He would hike into town on Sunday, work that week laying new rails and then hike back to the farm with a load of flour or other provisions on his back the following Saturday night.

Carsten was never content. He sold his first claim to his brother because he felt the soil was too thin, then he staked his second claim, and built a house on it. He leased land with purchase options and traded nearly everything; a wheelbarrow for 40 acres; a shotgun for 160 acres. He sold and bought land regularly.

This was rough, frontier country. The nearest trees were in the Loup River Valley, some 20 miles away.

Weather was always the deciding factor in farming. In winter, it was a question of survival. The Bosselman house was nearing completion on April 13, 1873, when an Easter Sunday blizzard swept down the Platte Valley. Carsten and Mary brought all their animals, including their oxen team, into the house basement. Comforters and blankets were hung along the walls to keep the snow from sifting in. They spent the next three days of the storm in bed, the only way to keep warm with their limited wood supply.

The following summer, and the summer of 1875, were grasshopper plague years. They tried to save their garden by covering plants with bedding, but the hoppers

The Oldenburg home of the Bosselmans. A farm family, the Bosselmans were used to hard work when they came to America. Their first stop was in Michigan, where Carsten learned how to dig out dozens of tree stumps--so many, in fact, that he decided to move to Nebraska where trees were more scarce.

This is the farm pond Carsten built in mid-Nebraska. He took great pride in nature and actually imported white-tailed deer and other wildlife not native to the region. His grove of trees bordering the farm consisted of 32 different varieties. Carsten was one of the first environmentalists in a harsh land.

liked to eat sheets as well as the plants. Everything was consumed.

Carsten was one of the first true nature lovers in the Midwest. He cared about plants and animals.

Both Carsten and Mary agreed: Summers were survival times, too, in this forsaken country.

Had they not invested all their money in the farm and home they would have immediately packed up and gone back to Michigan.

Carsten was also one of the first true environmentalists in Nebraska.

Carsten loved trees (despite his Michigan experience). He planted a 20-acre grove of 32 different varieties of them near the farmhouse.

A vegetable garden took more than three acres. Flowers were everywhere. He built two ponds with windmills and stocked them with fish, waterfowl, cranes, four different breeds of pheasants and all types of wildlife. He even imported Virginia White Tail Deer from his friends and relatives back east and put them on the property which he then called Deer Lake Stock Farm and invited his friends and neighbors to visit his oasis in the "Nebraska Desert."

Georgina Frauen's grandparents were good friends with Carsten and the family. They came over often on Sundays, after church, and enjoyed the "picnic grounds," as Georgina called the area. She remembers that the Bosselman girls, slightly older than she, must have spent days getting ready for the Sunday feeds.

One thing for sure. Central Nebraska never before or since, saw anything like the early Bosselman touch. Before Carsten, no deer had ever been seen this far west in Nebraska.

Brother Art recalls that Carsten really liked animals. One late fall day the ponds were getting ready for a freeze-over, thus trapping many of the hundreds of ducks still frolicking in the water.

Art built several cages near the windmill, considered the last place to completely ice up. The wild ducks were forced into the cages by the slowly freezing pond.

"We had them. Free duck dinners for a month," Art reported.

"Trouble is, Carsten sneaked out that night and set all the ducks free."

· The land kept Carsten busy until the end. The day he died, in 1923, he milked his three dairy cows, fed his wild animals and then said, calmly, he didn't feel well so he was going to lie down.

The father was never a man of the land like Carsten, but he knew law and business.

He went to the bedroom and died quietly, out of sight of everyone.

Fred remembered those days well, even though he was only six years old. The Bosselman family had lost their leader. Worms had lost the stalwart pioneer who knew everything.

Charles the Old was the only surviving son He took over the farm, then totaling nearly 1,000 acres.

He was never a man of the land as Carsten was. Charles was well-educated by standards in those days. He knew the law and he knew business. His studies 25 years ago in Grand Island's business school established him as a legal advisor to the German immigrant population in Central Nebraska. Charles performed his counseling chores enthusiastically and, most times, at no charge.

"He never should have been a farmer," Art said. "He only did it because he was the only boy and Carsten wanted him to do it."

After Carsten's death the ponds dried up, the wildlife escaped and the gardens went mostly unattended. But Charles the Old was always a smart farmer. He made money on the farm in days when many of the neighbors were going broke.

Fred heard his first cowboy and Indian story from a man who had been there.

The Reverend Schroeder had long left the community when Charles took over the Bosselman properties. He had been called to preach in a northern Wisconsin community early in the century. But the pastor returned to Worms, his creation, as often as he could. He was always welcomed as a speaker on special occasions. He had lifelong friends in Worms—and he had his favorite sister, Johanna, married to Charles the Old with five children of her own.

Pastor Dick was always rather proud of the marriage he, in effect, had arranged. He always allowed plenty of time to visit Johanna and Charles' children and tell them tall tales of the west.

Fred heard his first cowboy and Indian stories from the man who'd been there.

The peach truck now was rolling along in the bright, morning sun and Fred was thinking back to his childhood. He never could forget his first whipping. He must have been in the first or second grade. One day he crawled into the family's dog house to smooth down some straw he saw sticking out, and he suddenly decided it might be a good idea to burn some of that excess straw.

An average student, Fred liked everybody-- and they liked him in return.

He got a match from the house, lit the straw and then watched, horrified, as the fire, fed by a hefty south wind, leaped into the nearby cob house.

Everyone came running, Charles, Norman, Charlotte and his mother, but particularly did his father arrive with a bucket of water and a strap in hand.

Just as his father was about to bestow the punishment, his mother, Johanna, intervened.

"Charles, the boy was just trying to clean up the place. You've got to let them learn, too."

Charles the Older didn't stop. But as all the boys agreed later, the whipping wasn't as bad as some experienced before by his older brothers.

Fred was called Freddie in those days. Some of his school and farm chums—and his older brothers— still call him Freddie.

He was just an average student, always a couple of A's and B's behind Charlotte and Charles, the older sister and brother who led their classes.

But he was no dummy. He remembered one day he was the only one in his class able to spell the word "functional." The rest of the class had to stay after school—not Freddie.

"They thought I was pretty smart, mostly because I came from that smart Bosselman family," Fred joked later. "But really, I was just lucky that day—but I never let them know it, and I think that was pretty smart."

Edna Quandt characterized her schoolmate this way:

"Freddie was not aggressive. He liked everybody and he still does. Freddie goes out of his way to speak to you now, whether you're rich or poor, famous or not, and

The class picture at Zion Lutheran School, Worms, Nebraska, taken on March 5, 1924. Number identifications are: 1-Fred Bosselman; 2-Norman Bosselman; 3-Charles Bosselman; 4-Charlotte Bosselman; 5-Lillie Bosselman; 6-Esther Simonsen Van Pelt; 7-Edna Meyer Quandt; and 8-Art Luebbe.

The present school and church at Worms. These two buildings, plus the pastor's house, two residences and a cafe-bar are all there is to the town today, and it wasn't much larger in the 1940's.

he did then. A strange thing. Maxine is the same way."

One of the biggest influences in his life at that time, Fred recalled, was his teacher Paul Frese. Tall, somewhat fat, but a big promoter of physical fitness. He was also the strict disciplinarian. The rod did not rest lightly in his hands. On the other hand, if a child became sick or could not perform, Teacher Frese was tender and caring.

Most Worms people in those days were too tired to socialize much. They worked, ate and slept in that order.

It was his practice, when all students were seated in his fourth grade class, to begin dictating numbers as he walked to the rear of the classroom to close the door. The students were expected to solve problems as he talked. When he turned and walked to the front of the room, he would suddenly stop and tell the students to exchange papers for grading. He was not afraid to teach the Worms youngsters about parts of their bodies, either.

His brother was pastor of the Zion Lutheran Church at the same time. One year, during the depression, Teacher Frese came to the church elders and said they could not afford to hire two teachers that year. Normally Teacher Frese taught in the Big School, which took in grades 4 through 8. He volunteered to teach the entire school, including Little School (grades 1 through 3) and handle all 74 students at Zion Lutheran. No extra pay, either.

Fred thought back. There was not much socializing in those days. Everybody was too busy. And when you worked 12-and-more-hour days you were just too tired to do much else than work, eat and sleep.

The Bosselman family did have their Sundays, however. Mother Johanna and the two daughters, Char-

*The truck,
on a gravel
detour,
had a hard
time
making
some hills,
and it was
a scary trip
to Arnold.*

lotte and Lillie, set a full table for after church.

Often neighbors were invited, but never so many so as to add up to 13. Oh, there could be more—or less—but never exactly 13. Johanna was superstitious.

Art remembers that when he was number 13 he ate in the kitchen.

Sunday afternoons were reserved for ball games in the summer, sleep or study in the winter and, at other times, whatever mischief could be arranged around the place.

A certain number of rings on the party telephone line signaled a coyote had been sighted. That generally produced five or six teenagers with shotguns.

By the end of the winter hunting season, the youths would have collected 20 to 25 pelts. These were sold and the money spent on a picnic the next summer.

Fred was pretty much the community driver, he remembered. He handled the coyote hunts and he generally drove the car or pickup in the late 1930's when the guys went dancing.

He once took Arnold Dammann into Omaha with a truckload of cattle. They generally traveled Highway 30 because it was paved all the way. This time they tried Highway 92, a graveled road then but a straighter shot into Omaha. Besides Highway 30 had a lot of construction going on.

Fred's truck had a lot of trouble getting up the hills on Highway 92. On a couple of upgrades, Fred asked Arnold to get out to lighten the load, and, in case he had to back down, show him the way.

"That was one of the scariest trips I ever took on

the truck," Arnold recalled. "We must have tried a half dozen hills at least twice. We were all night getting into Omaha."

Wisconsin trips for calves were especially dangerous because of the roads and loads.

"Nothing to it," was Fred's answer. "If you want to get scared come with me to Wisconsin some time."

Fred made regular runs to Madison, Wisconsin, to buy dairy calves for resale in the Worms area. Arnold and the Dammanns were steady customers.

The Wisconsin trips were especially dangerous during the spring, when the double-decked trailer Fred was hauling would swing in the wind and on slick roads.

There was danger of another type on the Omaha trips. One night Fred was sitting in the restaurant of the old Hotel Miller in South Omaha after he had delivered his load to Armour's.

"Hello."

He heard the melodious voice in his ear.

A quick turn of the head revealed a young girl at the counter next to him.

"Hi."

"Anything I can do for you?" the girl asked.

"I don't think so."

"I saw you sitting here and I thought you might be lonely," she said.

"Just tired. I came in from Grand Island tonight."

"That's interesting. I know some people from Grand Island. If you want to have some fun I'll tell you about them and maybe we can do some other things."

"What other things?" Fred asked.

"Do you have money?"

"How much?"

"Five dollars."

"Too much."

The girl looked past Fred to a group of drivers sitting at a nearby table. One of the drivers was eyeing her. She concentrated on the man, got up and walked over to him.

After a brief conversation he got up and they left the coffee room together.

Fred, watching this, talked to one of his buddies at the counter:

"I think I know what she wanted, but she seemed a little too clean for that," he commented.

Fred, always the believer and trusting person, never did find out what that girl wanted.

~~~

There was a huge thump and the Ford lurched.

Fred sat up in an instant. He turned to Robert.

"What was that? A tire?"

"No, we hit a piece of wood. I couldn't turn off it because of the traffic," Robert replied.

"Let's stop and take a look," Fred suggested, and Robert wheeled the peach truck to the side of the road.

There was no damage, they decided, after Fred and Robert crawled under the fenders and looked over the undercarriage.

Fred counted the miles to Maxine when they began to get near home.

Ogallala was only 10 or 12 miles down the road. It was dinnertime, and Fred suddenly realized he was hungry.

The meal at the cafe on the main drag through town was filling, and Fred was glad to be finished and back on the road for home. Robert still drove. Fred counted the miles to Maxine.

They drove up to Charlotte and her husband, Al Eaton's place in Grand Island just about five o'clock. Charlotte had the bushel baskets ready. It took about a half hour to fill the 42 baskets Charlotte had promised to sell to her Grand Island neighbors and friends.

"These look great, Freddie," Charlotte was in an enthusiastic mood as they filled the baskets.

"Sure you and Robert won't stay for supper?"

"No. Maxine's expecting me," Fred was always low-key around his big sister. Otherwise, he knew her eagerness and selling abilities would overcome anything he wanted to do. In this case, he wanted one thing: to get home.

Charlotte was teaching school at Zion Lutheran in Worms again that year. She hadn't wanted to return to their old school, particularly since she had nearly 10 years of teaching experience in the Chapman and Central City school systems. But she had married Al a year and a half ago and the Central City school board had dropped her contract. Married people, it seems, were not priority hires in many school systems these days. So Charlotte took her enthusiastic ways back to Worms where she was greeted as she always had been: the sharp lady with big ideas who was really ready to work at anything.

Fred remembered when Charlotte was directing plays and she was still in school. Charlotte was always on a fast track.

"I think we can get two-fifty for these baskets," Charlotte said.

"Why not?" Fred knew it was useless to argue with Charlotte, even

Fred and Robert dropped off peaches in Grand Island, then headed the last few miles home.

though he could see some difficulties when neighbors
began comparing prices. He and Maxine would continue
to sell their baskets at $1.75 to $2, the price agreed upon
before Fred left for Colorado.

"Why don't you and Max get together?" Fred hoped
Maxine could keep Charlotte at the two dollar price.

Al and Robert had filled their baskets and were
chatting together near the truck's cab. Al, ever the
mechanic, was probably telling Robert why they shouldn't
depend on brakes in the mountains.

"Let's get moving," Fred told
Robert as he walked to the driver's
side of the Ford and opened the
door.

*People
were waiting
at the store
when the
peaches
arrived and
Maxine began
counting.*

The last 13 miles of the trip
went smoothly. Waiting for them
at the Bosselman place was Maxine
and a few neighbors.

"I passed the store coming
in," Fred said. "There were a lot of
people down there. Are they waiting for us?"

"We'll sell everything down there. I talked to Louie
and its all right," Maxine reported as she gave him a big
welcoming hug and a kiss.

Fred picked up Maxine, as he always did when he
hadn't seen her for a couple of days. He swung her around
a half-circle then gingerly set her down. She wasn't so
tiny anymore.

It wouldn't do to have anything happen to her now
when she was just a few weeks away from the birth of
their first child.

"You're putting on some weight, Maxie," he said.
"Sure you can handle this?" He nodded towards the truck.

Maxine always removed the bruised peaches on

top before the sale began.

"You and Robert take a couple of baskets up there and start filling them. I'll take care of things down here. Then we have to get into town," was Maxine's reply.

The day ended close to midnight when all the peaches were sold and the cash collected at the Farmers' Union store in Worms.

Maxine, who did the counting, estimated that there were close to 60 people at the peach sale. Sale receipts totaled $557.50, and there was lots of laughter and good times as neighbors kidded neighbors and Louie sold out his pop and hot dog supply in record time.

And the best story of all was when Fred told the happy group about his trip down the Colorado mountain..

Chapter 5

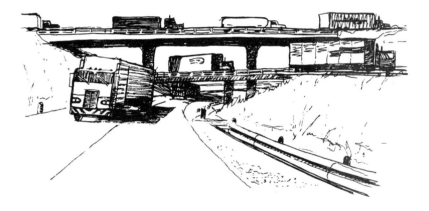

A ROLLING TRUCK MAN

On September 2, 1942, Barbara Ann Bosselman, the oldest of a
remarkable group of offspring, first
saw the world from the sterile con-
fines of St. Francis Hospital in Grand
Island, Nebraska. She was an 8
pound, 1 ounce bundle of noise, dark
like Fred but fine-featured like her
mother.

*No indoor
toilets, a
pump for
water and
a kitchen
stove to
help heat
the busy
first farm
home.*

It was a normal birth by all
standards, and Maxine and the baby
were both released in good health
the following Labor Day weekend.

The two-story frame house
Fred had purchased from his father, along with 200 acres
on the south side of the original homestead section, would
be home for the Bosselmans for the next six years.

There were no indoor toilets. A slow-starting wood
stove and a rusting hand pitcher pump for well water
graced the kitchen. Maxine's bed was a wedding present
she bought herself from Sears for $49, and older brother
Charles had donated a dining room set.

An old oil furnace smoked up the basement, with
its only vent in the living room. That vent would have to
take care of the heat needs of the first floor, which,
thankfully, included a bedroom. In winter, the Bosselmans
closed off the upstairs, where three more bedrooms were

The going farm wage then was $30 per month with free room and board.

located.

Fred's main goal that fall was to save enough money to buy some living room furniture.

"I never liked that house," he explained. "You had to go through rooms to get to rooms. The furnace was too small and always overworked. I never knew when it was through for the day or night, and like everything else, it always needed fixing."

Maxine looked on the old house, even with its inconveniences, as a first home, complete with a new baby. She was happy and busy. It was a start, not ideal, but something which could be improved.

At various times the young family had a hired hand staying with them. Fred kept 30 to 40 beef cattle and up to 50 hogs on the farm. The Bosselmans also handled a dairy herd of 14 Holsteins. Then there were grain crops and haying, always a summer full of 15-hour days.

Help came from neighbors and friends of the Bosselman family—people like Alfred Niemoth, Harold Kuck, Walter Kurz and Reuben and Elmer Niedfeldt. Fred could always find one of them unemployed for a week or two. He paid them all the same—$30 a month with free board and room. In winter, they slept in the unheated upstairs and ate their noon dinners with Fred, Maxine and Barbara.

Fred was busy on the farm in the mornings, but later in the day he nearly always found time to tinker with the Ford truck or take on a hauling job. The run to the Omaha stockyards became routine, as Fred had to schedule his livestock and grain hauls for neighbors, sometimes weeks in advance.

The little ones, Barb and Chuck, pose besides Dad's new airplane. The J-3 Cub was a classic, still used today. Fred traded this plane in on a Piper Tri-Pacer just a few years after this picture was taken.

A teenage boy handled the tractor power while the men threshed on a typical Midwest farm in the youngsters raced to 1930's. Note the horses at right. Farm women cooked piles of food for the neighborhood threshers and agile youngsters raced to the fields with water in the afternoons. *Photo courtesy Stuhr Museum of the Prairie Pioneer, Grand Island.*

Weekends during every June and July he made the trip to Wisconsin for dairy calves. He made the trip non-stop each way now, so he didn't have to use any so-called truck stop facilities along the way. He always remembered his first snore dormitory experience in Cedar Rapids and vowed to never give himself an opportunity to repeat it. This meant a 3 A. M. departure Saturdays and a seemingly never-ending drive over the narrow Iowa highways with their dangerous, inwardly-cupped edges. It was not a pleasant trip, even though Fred liked to drive. There was little rest when he arrived, and the return must be made on Sundays.

Some calf buyers loaded animals into the back seats of their cars, presenting interesting moments.

Fred always got a warm feeling inside when he was within a few miles of Worms. Like his coming back from the Colorado peach trips. There was always a happy crowd waiting for him. And, of course, Maxine.

He unloaded the calves at the farm and Maxine took the cash payments from eager, lined-up buyers.

"Some of those people buying calves didn't have trucks, so they loaded a calf in the back seat of their cars and drove away," Maxine recalled. Getting those sprawling legs inside while trying to close the car doors at the same time was an interesting action picture.

Things, including the human mind, weren't always so efficient in those days, either. Fred remembers building a 100-foot long hog shed, mostly by himself, and then, after it was completed, giving up raising hogs.

"That shed never saw a hog. It got a little embarrassing later on, but the hog market never did improve enough to restart 'em the rest of the time we were on the farm," Fred said.

*A day's work
for a buck
was the
usual pay
during the
depression.
There wasn't
much change
until World
War II.*

The dry and dusty depression days of the early and mid-1930's left Mid-America with a hangdog hangover. What was bringing a buck in 1934 seemed to still be bringing a buck in 1941 and '42. Corn pickers during World War II were making less than 5 cents per bushel. A hard day's work on another farm still brought around a dollar.

Fred remembered Art Luebbe's brother who owned 160 acres west of Worms. The brother decided to give up farming just before Pearl Harbor. Everything, including the house, its contents and all the land, was to go in an auction. Starting at 10:30 in the morning, the sale lasted into the night. It brought a total of $1,900. But maybe that wasn't too bad. Art's grandfather had picked up most of the land for $6 an acre, back in the 1870's. At least the brother nearly broke even.

Fred's brother, Norman, left for the service in February, 1942. Only a couple of weeks before, he had married a Worms' girl, Annetta Kuck. Norman was farming land leased from his father.

Charles, the only brother who was unmarried, pleaded with the draft board to take him instead, but there was no compromise before the farm exemption rule came in. Norman would have to go, and Charles and Fred would have to take over his 300 acres.

Norman spent his service years in an engineering battalion helping build the Alaskan Highway. He came home at the end of 1943 to stay, mustered out of the service for medical reasons. It seems Norman had suffered a particularly virulent and persistent strain of dysentary, impossible to shake. Eventually, he resumed his farming.

Norman's favorite expression during those days was "We used to not be able to talk about how tough things were on the farm because we didn't know anything different. Now I know something different, and I can say honestly—things were really tough on the farm."

Charles the Old still had regularly scheduled meetings with his sons, when they were home. But now, instead of learning sessions for the boys, they became information trading and story-telling meetings.

One of the pioneering Bosselmans was buried alive in a well he dug. His grave remains unmarked.

One of Charles the Old's favorite stories concerned the whereabouts of Claus Bosselman's grave, a family mystery for 50 years. Claus was Carsten Bosselman's brother and an early arrival in the Worms area.

One day before the close of the century Claus was digging a well in the front yard of his 160 acre claim. It was dinnertime and his wife called from the house.

"Just a minute until I finish this wall," Claus responded.

His wife heard no more for another 15 minutes, and she called again. No answer. She waited another few minutes, called again, and when she heard nothing but silence, she went outside to look. She found the well covered up, with Claus' shovel sticking out, and she knew what had happened.

Screaming, she began digging, but the ground was caving in around her, and she finally ran, still half-crying and screaming, to the neighbor's place more than a mile away.

The neighbors tried mightily to get Claus out, but

digging only produced more slides in the sandy soil. They finally gave up.

The group decided to bury Claus right there. They pulled out the shovel and put up a cross.

There was a rumor that Claus' body was removed later, but no one knows exactly where it is now. The grave marker disappeared long ago.

But the story has a happy ending. The Widow Bosselman continued living alone with her two children until a smart local widower noticed an obvious situation.

"You're living alone and I'm living alone. Why don't we get together?" was his simple marriage proposal. They raised another family.

Pigs in Clover dish had nothing to do with pigs or clover.

One of the early Bosselmans' favorite meals was Pigs in the Clover. Fred remembers helping to prepare it. The Bosselman girls were unexcelled in the kitchen, but they didn't want anything to do with this one. Fred explains:

"I realize there are other Pigs in Clover dishes, but this was how we did ours during the depression days in Worms.

"You hollow out a baked potato and fill it with butter. Then you clean a sparrow and stuff it in. Put it in the oven for an hour and a half, or whenever it smells good, take it out and eat. It's delicious."

Ellsworth Reeves, a former John Deere implement dealer in Central City, remembers Fred and Maxine well during those early farm years. He said he helped the Bosselman boys get rid of their then-ancient combine in 1943. A North Dakota farmer needed some extra threshing capacity. It was war time and nothing was available at the usual sources.

Reeves said he knew about the Bosselman combine, one of the earliest Case models. If he sold it for a good price he could get the Bosselmans a new Deere relatively easy, he thought. He did and everyone was happy except Ellsworth. His bosses felt he should be able to promote a deal like that every week.

Many of his customers would or could write only one check a year to suppliers.

"I probably carried Fred for a month or two when he was short of cash," Ellsworth said. "I did it for a lot of people in the 1940's and I got stiffed just once. And that one ended up back at Deere."

The only way an implement dealer could make money then was to carry his own paper and make early payment to the factory on behalf of his customers. Then the dealer collected the 5 percent bonus plus the customer carrying charges, he explained.

Many of his customers would or could write only one check per supplier per year, Ellsworth pointed out.

"You could tell pretty well who was good as far as credit was concerned. I'd see Fred working all day and driving a truck all night. And I'd see Maxine sitting out on the old hay baler they had tying those bales. You just knew they'd make it."

Ellsworth said he made a big hit with Maxine when he sold Fred a new, automatic hay baler a couple of years later.

Charles, the father, also told the story about how difficult it was to get around in the old days when nothing was marked and no direction or road signs existed. He was awakened one night by a rap on his bedroom window, and a voice out of the darkness asked, "Do you know where Herbert Schipmann lives?"

Charles looked closely, recognized the questioner and said, "Come on now, Herbert. You are Herbert Schipmann."

"Yeah. I know. Who are you? Where do I live?"

It was a dark night and Herbert had spent some time at the Worms tavern.

Fred was always the entrepreneur in those war years. One of the deals he struck early on with Wise Stewart of Chapman involved stripping blue grass seed from the Bosselman pastures. Fred bought a second hand stripping machine, put it behind a team of horses and bagged the seeds for sale to Wise.

"Those seeds went for $20 a bag once they left Wise's place," Fred said. "He only paid me by the acre harvested, but it was good income for us every spring."

Old boiler tubes, cement blocks made good money in backhauls for Fred during the war years.

On his regular cattle and grain hauling trips to Omaha Fred was always looking for loads going back to Central Nebraska. He found a real bonanza one day when he learned how well old boiler tubes could be made into fences and feed racks. The 3-inch diameter steel tubes came in 14 to 18-foot lengths. Farmers loved them, particularly at the prices Fred offered. He picked up the discarded tubes for next to nothing in Omaha. The back haul tubes were a real money-maker until his Omaha supplier caught on to their value.

Anything with a back haul potential was fair game. Fred found a market for cement blocks in St. Libory one time and he hauled them back for Harvey

Langrehr's place.

"The only bad thing about that was that I had to load and unload those gosh-darned blocks. They weighed around 30 pounds each," Fred said.

Fred and Maxine didn't stop going to dances after they were married, even though they missed many more than they attended.

Fred used rum to start a fire in his old wood stove. It worked better there than it tasted.

A little booze always helped Fred become more nimble on the dance floor. The only trouble was that during the war years whiskey was hard to come by. The liquor store owner began insisting that his customers buy a bottle of rum along with their regular booze. No one, but no one in the Worms area, drank rum. Fred found a use for it, however. He saved it for starting fires in the wood stove.

Towards the end of the war Fred became interested in owning an airplane. He and Amos found a new J-3 Piper Cub, a fixed-wing two-seater with stick controls and 65 horsepower, at the Grand Island airport, then still an Army Air Force Base. The price was $2,340, a real bargain in those days. Fred had learned to fly in just such a plane. His urge to fly probably had something to do with wartime pilot heroes, but Fred only acknowledged he wanted to try another transportation dimension.

"It isn't much different from driving a truck," he always said. Maxine always took the flying bit with a "whatever makes him happy" philosophy. Later she joined enthusiastically in flying all over the country with Fred, but in the early days she was just content when he got down.

She didn't know about the morning he took up the Cub, and after reaching cruise altitude, he cut back the throttle to normal rpm. The engine promptly quit, and Fred circled back for a power-off landing.

He looked over the engine, found nothing amiss and fired it up again. Everything normal. So off he was, skyward again. The same thing happened; the engine went dead when he reduced power. Fred came in for a dead stick landing once more.

This time Fred began taking apart the carburetor. He could see nothing wrong. So he reassembled and pulled the prop to start the engine one more time. And then he heard a small noise like air escaping. He killed the engine and discovered that the gas gauge wire attached to the float lid of the carburetor had frosted over, allowing no air to enter and causing an automatic fuel shut down.

Fred cleaned the wire and never had any more trouble with that airplane.

~~~

Contacts with the trucking industry were growing for Fred all through the war years. His regular trips to Omaha and his aggressive search for back hauls helped establish his reputation as a hard-working, honest trucker. All it took from there was a surging transport industry. Fred rode that wave well.

Fred could almost feel the trucking industry take-off. He read President Roosevelt's letter to owners and drivers of trucks reminding them that the nation's five million trucks were a vital part of the war effort. And he heard about the Red Ball Express, a 400-mile system which ran from Normandy in France to the rapidly advancing front lines in Germany on parallel, one-way routes.

The trucking industry really took off after the war. Fred was part of that growth.

Leading the final victory assault

This was a new wrinkle in the 1940's, when hauling petroleum products was a matter of getting as much product as you could into limited capacity. The tandem trailer offered a compromise, adding bulk delivery potential.

One of the first Herman Oil Company stations (above) in Fremont, Nebraska. It was from here that Mabel Herman and her family got into the fuel transport business. (Right) Mabel Herman, a savvy business lady, took over after her husband's tragic death, raising two boys and a business to success.

Founding Mother

Mabel Was Her Own Movement

by Betty Stevens
Sunday Journal-Star, Lincoln, Neb.
Reprinted with permission

Fremont—Mabel Herman said she only did what she had to do.

But in the doing, she was at one time the only female petroleum products transporter in the nation and had a larger volume of business than anyone else in Nebraska.

Herman helped organize the Nebraska Transport Carriers (now the Nebraska Motor Carriers' Association) and the American Trucking Associations and was the only woman on both boards.

Herman's business evolved from Herman Oil to Herman Oil and Transport to Herman Transport and finally to Herman Brothers when she sold the business to her sons, R.L. "Dick" Herman and Dale "Tink" Herman in 1952. At the time of the sale, Herman Transport employed 125 people and had 25 trucks.

Herman, now 89, did not need a liberation movement to front for her. She *was* a movement.

Widowed at 30 with two sons and a mother to support, she inherited a bulk plant and the mortgaged and wrecked delivery truck in which her husband died. The year was 1930.

A brother-in-law, Claremont J. Herman, then 22, came from

Continued on page 44

(Above) Herman in 1940; (below) At her service station.

was General George S. Patton who said, "The truck is our most important weapon."

In 1946 Fred made the big step. He bought an L. J. Mack tractor and a barrel trailer, designed to haul liquids. Earlier, he visited Mable Herman in Fremont and sold himself as the person who could deliver the outstate Nebraska market to the state's pioneer petroleum hauler, the Herman Oil Company.

Herman Oil Co. entered the picture as a hauler of petroleum products. Fred bought an L. J. Mack to open new territories.

Fred and the Hermans made a deal. Using the Herman name, he would supply jobbers and retailers in Central Nebraska with oil products stored in bulk pipeline terminals in the Omaha area. Herman would handle billings and collections and keep 10 percent of the hauling fees.

He showed Mabel and her sons, Dick and Dale, his new rig, capable of hauling 5,800 gallons. Dick, just returned from the service, looked over the Mack and pronounced it a gas-eater, probably uneconomical for petroleum hauling. The Hermans had just purchased two Internationals. They were proud of their choice.

Fred had some doubts himself about the Mack. It was a heavy piece of equipment. But it was too late to change now. He began hauling gasoline out of the Council Bluffs terminal for bulk storage tanks in Grand Island and North Platte.

Fred made the round trip from Grand Island once per day. He lined up two Grand Island drivers, Reuben Frei and Alfred Niemoth, to continue the cross state haul into North Platte.The Mack performed beautifully. Even Dick Herman had to reluctantly admit that he was wrong on its gas consumption.

Mabel Herman became the prototype of women's rights in business. She did it all after the tragic death of her husband.

Fred rapidly became a key link in the Herman oil delivery plan. He and Mabel Herman got along well. Since the sudden and tragic death of her husband in 1930 in a tank wagon fire when the family's oil jobbing business was only six weeks old, Mabel was motivated.

It took her a couple of years to learn the oil transport business and to figure out how to handle everything including caring for her two sons, then nine and five years old. It took courage to enter a male-dominated business world of heavy competition and hard physical labor. Mabel did it, and Mabel prospered through change.

By the late '30's, Herman Oil Company expanded from one small bulk plant and one station in Fremont, Nebraska, to the ownership of a 60,000 gallon storage plant, two stations and the management leasing of three others. The Hermans also had prestige, Fred recognized.

After 1934 Mabel began using more truck transport instead of rail. She quickly saw the potential in petroleum hauling. She took over two other competitors and "grandfathered" her young company into a contract carrier. She became immersed in the trucking business, and almost overnight found herself one of the few regional experts in liquid transport.

Here's what the August, 1937 issue of the <u>Petroleum Transporter</u> has to say about Mrs. Herman's organizational abilities:

"Fremont is located 137 miles north of the Kansas port of entry at Marysville. Her six drivers all headquartered at Marysville. Two drivers are assigned to each outfit, one of whom is named 'head man' and who has charge of the operation and care of that outfit. The 'head man' always drives the north or Nebraska end of the run so that he can contact the jobbers served, or Mrs. Herman, when necessary.

"One driver is the (super) head man for all three outfits. He has charge of the hiring and firing of drivers for the whole crew. He also routes the transports, keeps the driver's payroll records and brings the loads into Fremont to the Herman Oil Company, so that he contacts Mrs. Herman about four or five times a week to receive instructions and orders from the home office.

"At the end of each trip, a complete report is mailed to Mrs. Herman, showing every item of expense on that trip, the mileage covered, the amount of gasoline and oil used, as well as any information or incident pertaining to the operation. This is done before the drivers receive pay for that trip. These reports are carefully reviewed by Mrs. Herman and recorded in a master book.

"At the end of each month, then, a complete recapitulation of the operation of each unit is taken and averages are figured relative to the cost per mile of operation, the miles per gallon traveled and the actual net profit of the operations.

"If there is a decrease in the cost per mile, the drivers are commended highly, but if there is an increase the driver must show reasonable cause.

All details, reports are filled in before a driver gets his pay.

"The personal responsibility of each driver and the natural pride that each crew has in their own transport, makes them vie with each other in economy of operation and perfection of service."

Pickup points for the Hermans were Kansas terminals or refineries in Eldorado, Potwin, Arkansas City, McPherson and Wichita, the article continues, and with the relay point at Marysville. "This resulted in driver duty of 12 hours on and 12 hours off." The article goes on:

"Mrs. Herman personally takes care of all important business transactions relative to the transporting and oil jobbing business. She solicits the business and signs transportation and dealer contracts with other jobbers. She buys equipment and gives orders for its repair and upkeep. She has made a thorough and practical study of motor transportation and has her own ideas concerning the more technical points of the operation."

The Petroleum Transporter issue pointed to Mrs. Herman's Program of Service for Customers and said it "defies the best competitor."

Jobbers knew how much capacity Mrs. Herman's transport fleet contained, unit by unit. Any changes were made known to them immediately.

The jobber then could order exactly what he needed and he knew exactly how much he would pay for it. Cards for ordering and "cash on delivery" incentives were other features of the Herman service. The magazine said Mrs. Herman personally investigated all customer complaints.

Customers always knew how much was coming at what price. And service was primary.

"At regular intervals she writes each jobber-customer and encloses a questionnaire regarding the services rendered, which the customer fills out and returns," the magazine reported. She had a personal call schedule, too, it added, quoting Mrs. Herman: 'We are not going to cut prices. We are going to sell service. Everything is done with the jobber in mind.'

The magazine concluded: "Mrs.

Herman's enthusiasm over the motor transportation of petroleum products fairly bubbles from her conversation.

"Many times she has ridden all night on one of her own transports, then reported at the office for regular work in the morning. She reluctantly admits that she has 'even driven one of them.'

"Here is a striking example of a modern business woman practically 'showing the way' in a field that heretofore the men might have considered strictly their own."

Even though she turned the operation of her company over to her sons in her later life, Mabel Herman remained the Grand Lady of the petroleum transporters until her death in 1991. Fred Bosselman and Mrs. Herman operated so much alike—neither paying much attention to the hours they worked—that they got along famously, even, as Fred said, "After the several times I had to sit in the Herman outer office waiting for a check."

By the end of 1946, Fred could see that his future was not in farming, even though he loved the land, its challenges and the mostly silent people who often scratched for a living off it.

Fred and Mrs. Herman paid no attention to the hours they worked. They were much alike.

He was too good at dealing and fixing things mechanical. And he loved driving a truck, though by now he was mostly supervising his hired drivers. He still took a load whenever he could. And he always filled in if a driver didn't show.

All of the Bosselmans took their more difficult mechanical problems to Al Eaton, their brother-in-law, and a talented Grand Island mechanic. In 1940, Al had married Charlotte, the older sister and school teacher. An Iowa n, Al was on his own at age 12. His father had died; his mother remarried a Sac City, Iowa, farmer, and Al didn't want to be on a farm any longer. So he left, traveling west.

As Al tells it, he stopped in Grand Island because he "got to know this girl, not Charlotte. The girl didn't last—it was a quick marriage and an even quicker divorce--but Grand Island did."

He began working as a mechanic in a downtown garage. He met Charlotte through a mutual friend; Charlotte's car needed fixing.

Al took an immediate liking to the intense and bright Charlotte, as he did to the entire Bosselman family. He and Charlotte were often guests at Fred and Maxine's. They went to the farm to visit Charles the Old and Johanna more frequently now that Charlotte's father was getting older and even more infirm.

As did many Grand Islanders, Al worked at the nearby Cornhusker Ordinance Plant during World War II. Charlotte was teaching school in Central City, 30 miles to the northeast.

"I got lazy at the ordinance plant," Al reminisced. "But I got interested in truck mechanics out there, and sure enough, when Freddie got in trouble with his Mack, he came to me as one of the few guys around there who could handle heavy engine maintenance."

Al, Charlotte and Fred saw what was happening; they wanted to talk to Charles about a truck stop.

Fred and Al couldn't help but notice the increase in trucking and road building in the area. Most of the roads were still not hard-surfaced at the end of the war, but more all-weather improvements were going in—and there were good indications this trend would grow rapidly in the nation's hoped for,

September 1, 1973 is another milestone in our lives. This is the day we turn over ownership of Bosselman & Eaton, Inc. in Grand Island to our brother and brother-in-law, Fred Bosselman. We are delighted to have Fred and Maxine and their family back on East Highway No. 30.

September 1 marks the date of our retirement — or semi-retirement — from a business that has not only been near and dear to us for 25 years, but one that has been very good to us. Through the years there have been sorrows and joys, hard work and fun, disappointments and success. To sum in word, though, it has been a pleasure.

It has been a pleasure working with and for the people who are so close to us, the people in the trucking industry, and the many who are associated with it.

How to say "thank you" in a special way, a different way, a sincere way is not all that easy. How do you tell all the people who have been so good to you over these many years just exactly how much they mean to you, how much you appreciate them? We wish we knew.

So, without all the fancy words, let us simply say "thank you all — you've been kind to us."

— Al & Charlotte Eaton

Charlotte and Al Eaton played key roles in the Bosselman family. Charlotte was an achiever, and after a full life of teaching school and taking care of an invalid father, she became a business woman. In later life Charlotte was active in civic and state affairs. Al Eaton was a knowledgeable mechanic who sparked the family's success at its first truck stop east of Grand Island on Highway 30.

This photo graced the cover of the Nebraska Motor Carriers magazine for many months. It shows, in exaggerated form, how truckers enjoyed the early interstate highway system. *Photo courtesy Nebraska Motor Carriers Association.*

post-war boom economy.

A cross-country road network was taking shape in the late 1940's, the predecessor of the interstate highway system to come 10 and 15 years later.

Fred, Charlotte and Al figured they wanted to be a part of the truck-use explosion. They decided to talk to their brother, Charles, who, they knew, was looking for land in Grand Island in order to build a small manufacturing plant, aimed at producing a couple of his farm inventions.

Chapter 6

THE START OF SOMETHING BIG

Charles Bosselman, oldest of the Bosselman brothers, always chose the less well-traveled roads in life. He was the innovator, the thought-leader and the man other people came to with their problems.

Like his father, he was handy with tools. He loved to experiment. He remembered the time in his early teens when one of the heaters in the chicken brooder house overheated. In those days you never threw anything away. You fixed it. And if that was impossible, you found some other use for the rebel part, even as a doorstop.

Nothing was ever thrown away in those days; it was fixed or used in some way.

Charles simply isolated the offending heater to a near corner of the brooder house, erected an asbestos wall around it and devised an alarm system that rang a bell in the house when the heater got too hot. It worked. Charles filed for a patent on his warning system the next year.

Bob Poland, a Grand Island oil jobber, appreciates what it takes to operate a farm and admires Charles' innovations.

"I heard that when he was 14 years old and his father took sick, Charles and the brothers bought an ensilage cutter for a failed corn crop. They had to have something that brought in cash in a disaster year, and

Charles convinced everyone that this machine could do the job.

"Lo and behold, that cutter kept busy the next two years. The Bosselman family survived, and even made money in bad times thanks to Charles' planning. And that's a good example of the whole family's spirit, too," Poland said.

The patent Charles held the longest without any action involved a dash-mounted tire pressure gauge.

"Never could figure why no one wanted it," Charles said. "Must be because there was so much other stuff on the car dash-boards.

No demand for a tire pressure gauge mounted on the dash, Charles discovered.

"Or, just maybe, it's because nobody really cared about tire pressures," he mused.

Charles did develop a clip-on tractor power take-off. Variations of the principle are still in use today. In the mid-40's, however, it was ahead of its time. Charles had enough acceptance, he felt, to go into manufacturing this item. Another product with potential then was irrigation splash boxes, used to direct water flows. Charles bought old powder cans from the Ordinance Plant and converted them for a growing number of irrigators.

The oldest brother also developed an interest in antiques. During the war, he had collected all types of interesting pieces from the estates of early Central Nebraska settlers. And his skilled hands did wonders in making them functional. It was basically a hobby, but he did sell some of the more worthy pieces to fellow antique lovers.

The year 1946 started badly. Charles the Old had not really been well for the past 16 years, when an attack

Charles, the oldest brother, was a great lover and restorer of antiques. A teak wood table that Charles used to own captures his fancy here in a home he and his wife, Elizabeth, owned for many years. Charles, in failing health, sold the home and nearly all of its collector item furniture and furnishings several years ago. Charles died in 1993. He is pictured below.

Charles, the father, died in 1946 following 16 years of handicapped living. Despite the fact that he could not get around easily, Charles the Old was a valuable legal and business resource to the entire Worms area.

of encephalitis nearly paralyzed him. Over the years he had regained some of the ability to care for himself, but he never could walk without assistance and simple tasks were often too much.   Through those years he directed farm activities from his chair, and he continued advising his neighbors on tax and legal matters. He never forgot how to use the knowledge he gleaned in the 1890's at Grand Island's business college.

Simple tasks were often too much for the father who had been ill much of the boys' young years.

Now, at 72, Charles the Old was reaching the end of his pioneering path. He couldn't keep his difficulty in breathing to himself anymore. He never complained, but each day was getting a little worse and he knew it and the Bosselman family knew it, too. They kept a watch at the homestead place. And they were there when Charles breathed his last on January 15, 1946. Fred remembered:

"I had to hold him up in his bed because his lungs were filling. He'd had a heart attack before, I know, but he wouldn't tell anybody.

"He just died in my arms that night. All of us were there. It was a simple death, without fuss or muss, and, in a way, in keeping with his life."

Charles the Old had left his mark. He was one of the organizers of the Farmers Union Cooperative in Chapman, Nebraska, and served many years as a member of the board of supervisors of Merrick County. More meaningful to his community was the constant support rendered his neighbors in free business advice and para-legal support.

His oldest son Charles and the farm's hired welder were producing their unusual mix of antiques and farm inventions in a Bosselman farm yard shed one day in

Charles was ready to get some space in town so he could manufacture some items he had invented.

October, 1946, when they were approached by a neighbor, Herbert Joseph.

Herbert sold insurance, and Charles was one of his clients, but he really was a frustrated real estate agent. Early on he saw which trade got the really big commissions. Herb was ready to reap.

"You ought to move this stuff into town, buy a building and go into production," he told Charles.

"I don't have any money," Charles responded.

"Now come on. I know better. You've got this farm. But you don't really need any. I tell you what. I'll find you a place in Grand Island you can buy at low dollar. Or maybe someone will sell you space in the back of their building. You may have to take a small loan on the farm, but that should be no problem.

"You got some good stuff here. You need to grow," Herbert said. "Could you use another couple of people?"

Charles allowed as how he could and gave Herbert the go-ahead to find him a plant or some land to start his manufacturing and processing. Within the next two years, Herbert brought back two possibilities. Both were in residential areas and both failed to get proper zoning approval by the City Council.

Charles remembered one Councilman saying, "We don't want Grand Island to be a dinner bucket town."

Charles figured they would have to find something not requiring zoning changes. And, sure enough, Herbert found 10 acres of land on the north side of eastbound Highway 30, just a half mile east of Grand Island's city limits. There was a motel and an eating place less than a half-mile down the heavily-traveled road, and another new motel just west.

The 10 acres were much more than Charles wanted and the price, $1,000 per acre, was like, as Charles said at the time, "Like I was going to build the Taj Mahal."

So Charles sat on it. And thought. Herbert was pushing him to take it, saying Charles could always sell off some of the 10 acres, and land prices were going up. Charles finally nodded and took the challenge. He bought the land and immediately started to erect a Quonset hut 60 feet wide by 120 feet long. It was early March, and the job went slowly, what with Charles and a pickup crew doing most of the work themselves in sometimes bitter weather.

Fred and Al Eaton approached Charles at just the right time. He was somewhat discouraged with the project. He wanted to do more with the property, but he didn't know quite what. When Al said he would move his garage from downtown Grand Island and Fred, Al and wife Charlotte suggested a truck stop with a restaurant, Charles wisely recognized the potential. Particularly if Charlotte would do the books and help with the restaurant.

"We can build it ourselves," Fred said, to cap the deal.

They formed a company with three equal shares. They borrowed $39,000, mostly from friends, and began their 15-hour construction days. The Quonset went up in record time and, at Charles' suggestion, they even put a brick and tile facing on it. They hired Alex Kalkowski, a local builder and friend, to help them construct a little restaurant and office next to the Quonset.

Once rolling, the Bosselman crew was unstoppable. They had everything working—"somewhat," Charles later admitted—in six weeks. They held their Open House,

Open House produced a big turnout at the new truck stop. Free coffee, doughnuts helped. with free coffee and doughnuts, on Wednesday, September 1, 1948.

"It was a huge turnout, bigger than we ever suspected. We must've had better than 500 people out there," Fred said.

Nearly two pages of advertising in the Grand Island Independent announced the event. The paper also carried a news story which, in part, said:

"A new Grand Island corporation, to be known as Bosselman and Eaton, Inc., will open Wednesday a half mile east of the city on the Lincoln Highway.

"The corporation will operate a complete service station, a general automotive garage and a cafe. It will also have the Central Nebraska Mack sales and service agency with a complete parts department to service any model Mack truck.

"Fred Bosselman will be the sales manager, A. W. Eaton, parts and service manager, and Charles O. Bosselman, station and cafe manager.

"The station and cafe will occupy one building and the garage and the Mack agency will be housed in a second building..."

Although there was little or no recognition of what exactly a truck stop was in those days, what happened in Grand Island then was mid-Nebraska's contribution to the birth of a new highway service industry.

Small roadside diners attached to one or two-pump service stations were a part of the road scene in America between World War II and the advent of the interstate system in the mid-1950's. All of them were alike—a place where a tired and lonely trucker could get

The first buildings at the Highway 30 truck stop were not impressive. But they were functional, and it was from here that the Bossselmans got their start. Business was good for the Grand Opening in September, 1948.

Fred Bosselman as a 12-hour-a-day pump jockey and cash register teller. There were no chairs in Fred's office; in fact, he was seldom there himself. Customer service meant more to Fred than maintaining an office.

a bite to eat and a tank full of gasoline, and that was about it. The
trucker was lucky when the all-night
operation wasn't located in the center of town but on the outskirts where
he could reach it without waking up
everyone not used to hearing heavy
motors and squeaking brakes in the
middle of the night.

Early truck stoppers planted their feet against the door so they were awake if anyone tried to enter.

Oran Jarrell of Virginia, one
of the nation's pioneer truck stop
operators, talked about his early
years:

"I started in 1944 on U. S. Highway 1 in southern
Virginia. In those days we ran 12-hour shifts and slept on
a cot in the office. That way, if anybody ever wanted
something for which they were paying us money, we'd
always be right there, day or night, whatever time of the
day."

Oran generally kept his feet propped up against
the inside of the front door. That way he was alert if
someone tried to get in during late night or early morning
hours.

Not too many truck drivers hung out at the Tic
Toc, which is what Oran called his place. It had no
showers, no sleeping rooms and not even a good-looking
waitress. In that sense, the Bosselmans led the pack.
They had their womenfolk in the kitchen and restaurant
areas and they generally had one of the men taking care
of the service end.

Business at Bosselman-Eaton was solid, almost
from the start. It helped that Al Eaton brought his
customers along. Fred's Mack agency wasn't setting any
records, but it wasn't dying either.

"We made some early sales to highway construc-

A competitor said 'Those farm folk will head back to the hills within a year.' He didn't know about family loyalties.

tion people, who seemed to like the Macks because they were heavier and more rugged than most of the over-the-road stuff," Fred explained. He was on the road, still a trucker, most of the first year of the new enterprise. But within two years, he became the "full time" service station operator at Bosselman-Eaton.

Not everyone wished the Bosselmans well. One downtown cafe operator predicted "Those farm people will head back to the hills within a year."

Although everyone in the family willingly pitched in for work, frictions did develop. At times, Charles felt he was holding the entire operation together by himself. Charlotte, after spending a day in the kitchen and a night on the books, had her own ideas about who was really running the place. Al kept busy with his mechanics and Fred was drawn into the operation more and more.

Here's how Charles described it:

"For the first year or so I was in charge of the whole place and taking care of the farm, too. Charlotte would help in the kitchen. She was a good cook. Maxine and Sister Lillie would bake and clean and Freddie pitched in when he came off the road.

"Al really held the place together in those early days because he had a built-in customer base which he brought along with him from downtown.

"I was counting our money one day and I realized we really weren't getting anywhere. Freddie and Al and I were each drawing $250 a month from the business—and that was too much load to pull.

"So I called a meeting. I said I would go back to the farm and Freddie would get off the road, sell trucks from the office and handle the service station end. Charlotte would manage the restaurant and do the books."

'You could turn around in the kitchen if you were careful,' Maxine said. The customers were crowded, too.

Maxine remembers she ended up as a part-time dishwasher and hostess, a general fill-in person and an odd-hours baker of pies and cakes. Lillie was the volume bakery goods producer, however. She would bake 50 to 60 loaves of bread, pies and roll pans each day.

The restaurant had four tables and seven stools, seating 26 very crowded people, or, more likely, 18 just simply crowded people. Maxine describes the kitchen as a place "You could turn around in if you did it very carefully."

Gasoline selling almost came as an afterthought. No one had bothered to seek suppliers in the heady days of constructing the buildings. Now it came time to find out which oil company was interested. As it happened, none of them were.

Charles, through a long siege, finally interested Mobil and their Flying Red Horse. No one really wanted what they considered to be at that time a "no demand" brand, and the Bosselmans called in their connections. Maxine's dad was a Standard agent in York and the Schroeder family in Omaha, related to Johanna Bosselman, their mother, had connections with Phillips 66.

As Fred describes it, "This was no bidding war. The way they talked and the way we learned it from them, we were lucky to have anybody interested in

Gas prices in 1948 were 12 to 15 cents a gallon. Diesel was 8 cents. Fred didn't use a chair and spent 12 hours on and 12 on again.

selling us gasoline. We were country kids and we believed them. So when Standard finally consented, we had a celebration."

Four pumps were installed. The service station business began. Prices ranged from 12 to 15 cents per gallon for regular.

"I would spend 12 hours on a shift, and then, when my relief didn't show, I'd spend another 12 hours down there. By that time, my regular shift was due, and I'd spend another 12. Nobody would believe it today, but that's how we did it then," Fred said.

Fred had time to enforce his own rules on service station operations. No. 1 rule was—no chairs. He saw too many people sitting down in stations, he explained, and he wanted none of that where he worked. As a consequence, Fred and any visitors to his tiny office sat only on top of his desk. If Fred took a nap, that's where his body was sprawled.

~~~

Fred and Maxine had two children by this time. Little Charles, called Chuck from birth, came along three years after Barbara. The young family was growing. It also was time to move off the farm and settle where the primary jobs were.

In the fall of 1948, the Bosselmans moved to a four-room house at 624 East Ashton Avenue in Grand Island. It was a small, stucco house with a small yard, but it was cheap.

"We picked up a veteran's defaulted 3.75 percent

The restaurant at the new Bosselman-Eaton stop was an immediate hit. All of the Bosselman womenfolk pitched in to help and the result was that the cafe was expanded twice during the early years, finally reaching a seating capacity of 125 during the 1970's. The restaurant still is a popular eating and coffee rendezvous point in eastern Grand Island.

This was the family's first home in the city. The Ashton Avenue home had four rooms, two crowded adults and two children--but if the space wasn't right, the price was. Fred bought it for $7,000 in 1947.

loan. The house cost a total of $7,000," Fred explained. "And I really didn't go for that place! I always wondered why I bought it. There just wasn't enough room."

Maxine said she was too busy to bother. She put Barbara in their bedroom and Little Chuck slept in the living room. She baked in the kitchen.

"No wonder I spent so much time at work," Fred commented.

"I guess I never really liked that house either," Barbara said. "I did like where it was located—not too far from the Saddle Club and the horse pastures of east Grand Island. I used to hang out with the horses."

One thing did bother Barbara: "It was when they told me I'd have to start in kindergarten rather than in first grade. I was six years old and proud of it. I thought I was too old for kindergarten."

~~~

During those years, there was no other truck stop in Grand Island, or, for that matter, in Central Nebraska.. But that didn't give the Bosselmans much of an advantage. They still had to deal with hard-nosed corporations, interested only in the bottom line return on their fuel purchases.

Bosselman's Highway 30 stop was the first in the area, but there were troubles, too.

"I remember we had one big user who wanted a kickback of a penny a gallon bought at our station, and we gave it to him," Al Eaton said.

Otherwise, it was a "pay-the-price-posted" world, Al added.

There were troubles, too. Fred remembers one slugging incident he had with a driver-customer whose truck was being fixed by Al. Fred recounts:

"The guy comes in on a Sunday morning, when I'm

fixing a tire. He's obviously drunk, and he starts accusing me of not getting his work done on time. He was cursing and calling me all the names in the book.

"I tell him I don't know anything about his job and that he'd better watch his language. He starts swinging. I duck and slug him in the mouth with my right. His false teeth break and he starts bawling. I don't know what to do, but I get him out of there and take him back to his motel room. I'm really nice to the guy considering what happened.

"The next day we hear from his boss. The boss says I picked on his man and hit him with a tire iron. He said his company would buy nothing more at our place. Then he hung up.

"We never did get that business back—at least, not for a long time. Maybe it's just as well. But I did learn something. No more am I ever nice to people who swing at me and then lie about it."

Fred used to service cars and trucks from the bare ground gravel and rock area between the two Bosselman-Eaton buildings. It was tough on his back, he admitted.

Getting under cars and trucks with your back to the bare ground was not Fred's idea of fun.

And so the first improvement to the property after Fred took over the service station operation involved laying concrete over the gravel area. The concrete pad also gave Fred and Al another light repair and maintenance station, if only for use during good weather.

Bosselman relations with other petroleum products people in the state were always excellent. The Hermans leased a building from Bosselman-Eaton, and Standard eventually awarded them jobber status. Fred also hauled for Abe Gendler's Liberty Gas and Oil out of Kansas City.

Just up the road was Francis (Fritz) Woodward whose folks operated a motel, service station and cafe for many years. Fritz even ran a transport out of Cheyenne, Wyoming, in direct competition with Fred's operation out of Omaha and Council Bluffs.

"The Bosselmans are wonderful people. You can always argue with them, but you'll not have any trouble from them. I never considered them competitors, even though we were the only ones on the eastern edge of Grand Island when they came out here after the war," Fritz said.

The first diesel fuel pump at Bosselman-Eaton was installed in early 1949, just after the Great Blizzard of that year paralyzed the state.

"We put it in because we had to, not because we saw an opportunity," Al Eaton explained. "We charged 8 cents a gallon, and our diesel business really took off." There was no tax on diesel fuel at that time. Now it's 40-plus cents per gallon.

Al didn't really welcome the extra burdens diesel engine repairs put on his shop, but he had no choice. He and Fred learned about diesel engines together at the time this motive power became a major factor in the Midwest's rapidly-growing trucking industry.

Diesel fuel demands came on in the late 1940's, and Bosselmans were forced into the servicing of engines.

Fred's connections with the petroleum haulers and the Hermans helped, too. In the winter of 1948-49 he still was making his trips to the pipeline terminal in

Fred nearly loses it all on a blizzard fill-in trip in 1949. He delivered the fuel to a snowbound station. Council Bluffs and passing on part of the big trailer loads of fuel to North Platte.

One night just after the New Year, his North Platte run driver reported sick (Fred always had his suspicions about this). He was the only one left to take the load. It called for delivery to Stapleton, Nebraska, about 30 miles north of North Platte in the Sandhills. The date: January 6, 1949. The first week of the Great Blizzard.

It had been snowing almost without stop for three days and nights and the only road open westbound was Highway 30, reduced to one-lane traffic. It began snowing again when Fred started his westward haul. At North Platte he dropped part of the load at a bulk storage tank. Then he turned the rig north, determined to finish his run. By this time, he couldn't see the road and he should have stopped, he realized later. The cold smashed at his truck and numbed everything on his body. Snow drove its way into the cab. It stacked in mounting layers on everything that wasn't moving. Outside and inside it was ravenously cold and not getting any better. Fred drove on, guided by the reflective markers on the side of the road though he was having more difficulty seeing them even as he dared to penetrate that blinding maelstrom.

He really was in Stapleton before he knew it. He turned gratefully into the service station to deliver his load. He knew the station was on the main drag, just as you entered town. Even so, he had to get out of the cab and feel for the driveway. He made the turn and ran smack into another problem—no one was home. Nobody was on the job. A station deserted. The world stopped by a

The 1949 blizzard paralyzed the Midwest for nearly a week. Shown here and on overleaf are just a few of the problems of digging out. *Photos courtesy Omaha World-Herald.*

BOSSELMAN AND EATON, INC.   EXHIBIT A
GRAND ISLAND, NEBRASKA

BALANCE SHEET
As of September 30, 1950

ASSETS

Current Assets:

Petty Cash Fund		350.00	
Cash in Bank		540.02	
Accounts Receivable		13,125.27	
Notes Receivable		749.00	
Inventories:			
Parts and Cafe Supplies	7,836.11		
New Mack Trucks	22,867.94		
Used Trucks	200.00	30,904.05	45,668.34

Fixed Assets:

Garage Equipment	5,237.96		
Cafe Equipment	3,818.70		
Service Station Equipment	5,951.78		
Garage Building	18,964.65		
Cafe and Station Building	10,842.77		
	44,815.86		
Less—Reserve for Depreciation	6,727.34	38,088.52	
Land		10,000.00	48,088.52

Other Assets:

Prepaid Insurance	142.91	
Good Will	4,000.00	4,142.91
Total Assets		97,899.77

LIABILITIES AND CAPITAL

Current Liabilities:

Accounts Payable	14,646.69	
Notes Payable—Current	1,360.00	
Universal C.I.T.	20,590.00	
State and Local Taxes Accrued	351.17	
Unemployment Compensation and Federal Excise Tax		
Accrued	317.91	
Social Security Tax Accrued	249.42	
Withholding Taxes Accrued	681.20	
Federal Income Tax Accrued	200.81	38,397.20

Long Term Notes Payable: 18,400.00

Reserve for Federal Income Tax: 1,597.21

Capital and Surplus:

Capital Stock	27,300.00	
Earned Surplus	6,858.16	
Increase in Surplus 1-1-50 to 9-30-50	5,347.20	39,505.36
Total Liabilities and Capital		97,899.77

ORIN CONTRYMAN
THIS REPORT HAS BEEN PREPARED WITHOUT AUDIT, UNLESS OTHERWISE NOTED.

The 1950 balance sheet and operating statements showed the Bosselmans largest money-makers were the restaurant, the service station and the garage, in that order. It was a time of growth, and although the profit returns weren't huge for the amount of work done, the enterprise was healthy and getting healthier.

BOSSELMAN AND EATON, INC.　　　　　　　　　　EXHIBIT B
GRAND ISLAND, NEBRASKA
STATEMENT OF OPERATIONS
For the Period January 1 to September 30,
1950

			Percent
Service Station Income:		91,399.85	100.0
Less—Cost of Sales—Service Station:			
Inventory 1-1-50	834.56		
Purchases of Gas, Oil, & Supplies	82,983.13		
Salaries—Service Station	3,828.53		
	87,646.22		
Less—Inventory 9-30-50	2,794.56	84,851.66	92.8
Service Station Gross Margin		6,548.19	7.2
New Mack Truck Sales:		48,401.82	100.0
Less—Cost of New Mack Truck Sales:			
Inventory 1-1-50	6,644.74		
Purchases of New Trucks	60,233.07		
Selling Expense—Trucks	400.67		
	67,278.48		
Less—Inventory 9-30-50	22,867.94	44,410.54	91.8
Margin on New Mack Trucks		3,991.28	8.2
Used Truck Sales:		17,985.00	100.0
Less—Cost of Used Truck Sales:			
Inventory 1-1-50	300.00		
Purchases of Used Trucks	16,047.95		
	16,347.95		
Less—Inventory 9-30-50	200.00	16,147.95	89.8
Margin on Used Trucks		1,837.05	10.2
Garage Income:		31,043.11	100.0
Less—Cost of sales—Garage:			
Inventory 1-1-50	2,535.40		
Purchases—Parts and Service	21,145.04		
Salaries—Garage	7,986.26		
	31,666.70		
Less—Inventory 9-30-50	4,782.59	26,884.11	86.6
Margin on Garage Sales		4,159.00	13.4

BOSSELMAN AND EATON, INC.　　　　　　　　　　EXHIBIT B
GRAND ISLAND, NEBRASKA　　　　　　　　　　　PAGE　2
STATEMENT OF OPERATIONS
For the Period January 1 to September 30, 1950

Cafe Income:		42,947.80	100.0
Less—Cost of Cafe Sales:			
Inventory 1-1-50	127.13		
Purchases of Cafe Supplies	23,140.57		
Cafe Salaries	11,480.58		
	34,748.28		
Less—Inventory 9-30-50	258.96	34,489.32	80.3
Margin on Cafe		8,458.48	19.7
Total Gross Margin		24,994.00	10.8
General Expenses:			
Executive Salaries	8,100.00		
Advertising Expense	547.85		
Depreciation	2,988.75		
Freight	400.34		
Insurance	887.46		
Legal Expense	154.00		
Lights, Gas, and Power	1,262.28		
Maintenance of Property	687.09		
Traveling Expense	294.61		
Office Supplies	401.65		
Taxes	1,390.08		
Telephone and Telegraph	543.36		
Transportation Expense	48.50		
Miscellaneous Expense	264.37		
Total General Expenses		17,970.34	7.8
Net Operating Profit		7,023.66	3.0
Non-Operating Items:			
Miscellaneous Income	602.21		
Interest Expense	631.46		
Net Business Profit		79.25	—
		6,944.41	3.0
Less—Provision for Federal Income Taxes		1,597.21	.7
Net Increase in Surplus		5,347.20	2.3

blizzard.

Fred knew it was useless to try to find help, so he idled the truck, cracked his window and fell asleep to the engine's soothing hum, almost all at the same time.

The next Fred knew was a thumping on his truck cab door. Or what he thought was the door. All he could see as he opened his eyes was white. Nothing but white. He stumbled out of the cab. Then he lost it all. He was out.

The service station people carried him into the station, stretching his body out on a work bench. A couple of minutes of fresh air and Fred was moving, putting his legs on the floor and walking. It was good they found him. Carbon monoxide poisoning is dangerous to your health.

Fred woke up with the biggest headache he never really wanted to know about.

"I'm okay. I'm okay," Fred kept repeating as he slowly tried to walk it off. "Can I get through to North Platte?"

"Maybe this afternoon."

It was the next day before Fred could start back.. When he did get back on the highway, he raced his truck back to Grand Island. The Hermans had installed a tachometer on the truck. It told them the exact mileage driven and the speed used.

He broke the speed record getting back because he wanted to spell his help.

Dick Herman looked at Fred's record later and remarked: "You've just broken every speed record between North Platte and Grand Island. I didn't know a Mack truck—or anything else— could go that fast in snow conditions on a one-lane, one-way highway."

Fred wanted to get back to Grand Island to spell his relief in manning the Bosselman-Eaton pumps.

The doors were always open at Bosselmans. One time the restaurant was closed for repairs; a free, big plate of sandwiches was left out for truckers.

The Bosselmans always believed a truck stop should operate 24 hours. Whatever it took to keep the doors open was done. Even if Fred or Maxine were called out of bed because someone didn't show. They were never too occupied or too sick. And if they couldn't make it because of family problems or an emergency, they always left a big basket of free sandwiches with hot coffee for their friends, the truckers. One time, when the restaurant was closed for remodeling, they supplied free treats, with an open door to the restaurant, for three weeks.

Fred was known to be something of a soft touch, particularly if it involved family.

He heard that another Standard station in Grand Island, run by Dick DeMers, was in financial trouble with Omaha headquarters. Fred had known Young Dick for several years and recognized him as a hard-working dealer.

Dick had five children. One day his wife evidently decided that was enough and left him with the kids to pursue her career in dancing. Fred thought this was a bad shuffle What was worse was the fact that Standard wanted to close Dick out right away.

Fred called the divisional offices in Omaha, followed through to Chicago and saved Dick's business. Not only that, Fred nursed Dick along financially for several years in order to get him solid again.

Two years had passed since the opening of

Bosselman-Eaton. The business was prospering. And Fred knew he, Al, Charlotte and Charles had made the right decision in 1948 when, on one cold February day two years later, he looked out of his cubbyhole office window and saw six semi's lined up to get to the Bosselman-Eaton pumps.

Those waiting trucks were beautiful!

Chapter 7

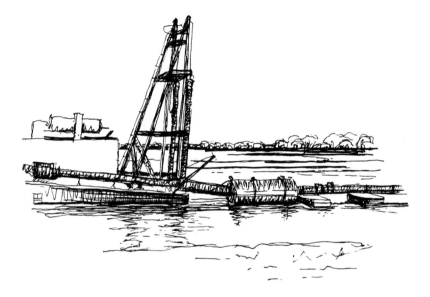

IS THIS A MOVE TO NOWHERE?

Tense was the word to describe the feeling in Fred's small office. Charlotte had just stormed through the door at full stride and she was angry.

Standard wanted payment with every load they delivered. Charlotte and Fred argued and won.

"I don't see why I'm writing checks to these bums three times a day," she shouted, waving her checkbook in Fred's face.

"Who's it for?" Fred asked, barely looking up from the pile of diesel fuel receipts he was thumbing through.

"Standard, the so-and-so's. They want a check for every delivery."

"That's ridiculous. Tell them we'll pay 'em once a week if they're nervous about it."

"Weaver said he's got to have payment on delivery. Omaha rules. You've got to talk to them."

Earl Weaver was a driver-independent contractor for Standard who kept Bosselman-Eaton supplied with gasoline through the Council Bluffs terminal. He was a friendly guy, Fred knew, but not one to break regulations, particularly if they came from the people paying him.

"I'll talk to him again. Is he still here?"

"Yes. But we shouldn't have to do this. We get three or four tanks a day. Why should we have to write checks for each load?" Charlotte asked, calming now that someone wasn't pushing her. She knew that her brother was a person who could get things done. 'This should be his problem anyway,' Charlotte thought but didn't say.

Fred picked up the receipts, stuffed them into the desk's center drawer and moved his legs to the floor. He had been sitting on the desk.

"I'd ask you to sit down," he said in a sudden gust of humor, "except there's no chair in here. "

Without another word Fred strode out of the office and walked across the tarmac to the tank-wagon whose long hose line was still poked into the underground tank. Earl evidently had just finished a delivery. He was standing near the tank wagon cab.

Earl held up his hands. "I know what you're going to say, Fred. I'll call the office again."

"There's no gosh-darned reason we should have to write you a check 20 times a week, Earl, now is there? Tell 'em this time that I'm not going to pay until the end of the month," Fred said. "They know where they can reach me."

I'll pay you at the end of the month, not 20 times a day, Fred told Standard.

Earl wasted no time in calling his district supervisor in Omaha. The supervisor said "No way" in large sounding letters, and told Earl to stop deliveries to Bosselman-Eaton as of right now.

Earl saw disaster. B-E was his biggest customer, by far. He was sympathetic to Fred and Charlotte. But he couldn't help. He told Fred, and Fred, surprisingly calm now, said he just wouldn't take any more product from Standard.

"That should solve all our problems," he told Earl. Earl duly reported this to headquarters.

The next day—and every day after that—the Omaha office of Standard called Earl and asked if Fred was buying gas from him. Earl said "No. I've been told I'll lose my job if I do it without collecting."

"How's he staying in business?" was the next question.

"I don't know. He must be getting gas from someone else."

Earl suspected Fritz Woodward was supplying Fred, but he didn't say anything. Fred surely had sources he wasn't telling anyone about. And B-E was still doing a good gas business.

Alternate sources of fuel saved Bosselmans this trip, and a line of credit finally was established.

Another week went by before Standard broke. Omaha offered Fred the option of paying once a week, but Bosselman had to go to Chicago headquarters to get the line of credit finally approved.

Charlotte was happy again. Fred beat the system and Earl could survive. In fact, B-E, even in those early days, was one of Standard of Indiana's largest Midwest customers.

The early '50's were boom and growth times for Bosselman-Eaton. Business improved steadily as the restaurant and fuel business expanded.

The first big expansion occurred in 1953. Others were to come later, when the 26-seat operation eventually became a modern restaurant seating 150. Charlotte now had a firm hand on the food business. All of the women in the family—including little Barbara who was "nine years old going on 20," as one local observer put it after watching her washing pots and pans in the kitchen—put in their hours, too.

"I hated that job in the kitchen. I scraped plates and got every dirty job they could think of," Barbara said.

Barbara and Chuck were put to work early- and they're still around

"I sure wasn't treated like I thought the boss's daughter should be treated but that was okay," Barbara said. "I learned a lot. Charlotte was firm, but fair and always the teacher.

"I finally graduated to bus girl, and then to waitress when I was 16. I was making $5 for every 8-hour shift, plus tips, and that was good money then for a schoolgirl. When I look back now, it was good for me."

Barbara recalls her first summer as a waitress. "They pulled every trick on me the kitchen could think of. Plates were too hot to handle, orders deliberately mixed up and I always got the grouch tables."

Little Chuck was kept busy cleaning up oil cans and mopping floors in the service station.

"I remember only a little bit about the farm," he said, "but I'll never forget my early days at Bosselman-Eaton."

Chuck got started in the business early. He was barely out of kindergarten when he was handed job responsibilities. By the time he was eight, he had a regular post as service station assistant. He actually didn't wait on trade or do much of anything but help keep the place clean, but Fred wanted him to think of himself as a key man and assigned him regular hours, some of which he kept.

Both he and Barbara were also baby-sitters. Mary Margaret Bosselman came along about then, and Fred Jr., the youngest, was not far behind. By this time the family moved to a much larger house at 1806 West First Street, an older brick home where everybody except the babies and Fred and Maxine had his or her own bedroom.

Dr. John Easley, a neighbor and father of seven

Barbara, 14

Chuck, 12

The Bosselman Children

Mary, 5

Fred, 3

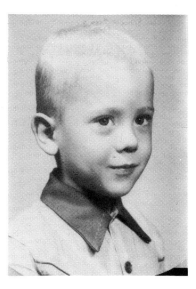

Fred and Maxine bought this older but larger home on First Street in Grand Island in 1953 and lived in it until Barbara and Gene bought it in the late 1960's. The house was torn down in the early 1970's to make room for stores, parking lots and an office building.

children who admitted that his family "just about populated the neighborhood," said he "didn't see much of the older Bosselmans—they were too busy. But what we saw we liked. And we sure had their kids around."

'A kind and gentle man' remembers Maxine baking through the night.

Maxine would be baking pies and cakes at three in the morning. Fred would be up all day and most of the night and had "horrible hours that only someone like Fred could handle. The kids pretty much had to take care of themselves—which they did admirably," Dr. Easley said. Now a widower, he remains a close friend of all of the Bosselmans. "A kind and gentle man" is the way they describe him.

Mary Margaret said she remembers a parade of baby-sitters and certainly her sister, Barbara, "who used to tell me all the time that I was adopted—especially whenever I would ask where my parents were."

The home on First Street eventually was torn down to make room for a shopping center and a savings and loan building. But not before the Bosselmans spent nearly 20 years of busy and happy times in its embrace.

"It's hard to tell friends I used to live on the parking lot of the Jack and Jill store, but that's what happened," said Lucille Martin, a long-time neighbor.

Bill Sassen, another former neighbor, said "Fred had a dream and he worked very hard, and his family also worked very hard to make that dream come true. They were great neighbors and good friends, and always will be close to us."

During summers Barbara and Chuck would spend days, even weeks, with their uncle Charles on the farm. He handled them well, teaching good manners and farm safety in about that order.

" I learned how to open car doors for women, what side to walk on and how to handle eating utensils from Uncle Charles," Chuck explained. Charles was still a bachelor then but as Chuck said, "He was good with kids. He took time and had the patience to teach the proper things."

Barbara remembers being chased by farrowing hogs after ignoring Charles' stern warnings to stay away from them. She and Chuck also got in trouble with an ugly-tempered ram and were rescued just in time by Charles.

It was all part of growing up in a smaller community, where a 10 minute walk would put you in the country. Good place to raise a family, Fred and Maxine agreed.

If there was a complaint from any one in the neighborhood it was because everybody in the Bosselman family seemed to be named the same. There were two Freds, two Charles.

"All we needed was another Max," said Mrs. Martin. Maxine had a response:

"In all honesty, I don't think I would name my kids again after their father or their granddad. It's just too confusing. But then, maybe after their mother?"

Never again will Maxine name her children after someone else in the family. But the beat goes on.

The confusion will continue, at least for another generation. Charles, Jr., Chuck's son who is now running Bosselman food operations, just named his first son Carsten.

None of the Bosselman children exhibited the spoiled child syndrome, according to neighbors and friends. They were put to work early and they learned the value of money by watching their parents, family observers said.

Forever forthright and direct, Mary said, "I know the family, particularly Barbara and Chuck, think Fred, Jr. and I are spoiled, but it's not so. Because we came later we may have had an easier time, but we still had to toe the mark, like everybody else."

Mary's husband Scott works Fred's farm at the old home place near Worms.

Both Mary and Fred A., as he is most often called by the family, went through divorces. Mary has since remarried, to a Wood River farmer, Scott Sahling, who now enthusiastically works Fred's farm near Worms. Fred, sometimes called Fred, Jr., has two children by his first marriage and keeps busy running Bosselman's wholesale, lubrication and transport divisions. He is known as a quick study with an outgoing personality.

~~~

Most of the truck stops of the early '50's were still "Mom and Pop" operations. A few, like Bosselman-Eaton, were swinging into the "whatever-you-need-we-got" era of total service, not only to truckers but to their communities.

B-E, for example, attracted large numbers of local resident diners, particularly on Sundays. Some of their customers would drive 30 to 40 miles for a Sunday dinner. And B-E became the place to go for weekday morning coffee and after hours snacks. It still is.

"We had kind of a neighborhood variety store out there," Fred said.

Verne Moseman, the Bosselman accountant and personal family friend for many years, recalls one of his first meetings at the Highway 30 property:

"Charlotte was really concerned about the short

Al doesn't solve the problem of short skirts, but he has a good time trying.

skirts some of the waitresses were wearing. In fact, she brought it up at the annual meeting.

She said, 'When some of my girls bend over, they're taking pictures of the entire crowd with their rear ends—and everyone is looking at the cameras.'

"She thought Al could solve the problem by sitting in a restaurant customer chair and then having the girls come in one by one and bend over in front of him. Those that failed to pass inspection would have to go home and change into longer skirts.

"Al willingly became censor. Not once, but on every shift for several days and nights. In fact, Charlotte had a hard time getting Al back to his garage.

"But Charlotte was never a person to be denied. Some of the girls had to change. The board meetings went on to less interesting subjects."

Moseman most often served as chairman at the annual stockholders meetings in those days. It was really a family affair, with the exception of Verne and Charles' lawyer and sometimes his accountant.

Charles brought his experts because he thought he was getting less than his share of the profits, Verne said.

"The only reason I was elected to chair the meetings was because no one could agree on who was the chairman, even though Fred was listed as president, Charles as vice-president, Al as treasurer and Charlotte as secretary. In fact, no one else wanted the job because there was so much bickering going on.

"Charles thought of himself as one-third owner and entitled to one-third of the income. He didn't really

Verne Moseman, now retired from public accounting, teaches business and accounting college level classes and serves on statewide regulatory boards serving the accounting profession.

Fred, oil can in hand as he services a truck at the Bosselman-Eaton truck stop, is quick to recognize that hard work and looking after the customers' interests pays off, no matter what business you're in. This photo was taken in 1951.

spend much time working in town because he was taking care of the farm. Charlotte and Al, between them, were spending 24 hours a day at B-E, and Fred was working at least 15 hours a day, seven days a week. They had salaries, which they thought were way too low and so they also had different ideas about revenue splits.

"My function was basically that of a referee. Charlotte kept the minutes, and they were reviewed by the company attorney, Franklin Pierce.

"I remember a lot of shouting and smoking tempers. One time I lost my cool and told Charles to sit down and shut up. He was old enough to be my father, but he did sit down and shut up—for a while.

Moseman was a referee at many of the board meetings. No one else wanted the chairman's job.

"Charles probably got mad at me during the meetings, but he never got mad at me professionally. He'll still call me up if he has tax problems."

The family may have had differences, but in the end they always stuck together and promptly forgot any quarrels, Verne noted.

Verne was a young CPA, just out of the University of Nebraska, when he first encountered the Bosselmans. He remembers being hired by the Contryman accounting firm in Grand Island for $180 per month and told to call on this little gas station out on Highway 30. The owners wanted help in filing incorporation papers and setting up books.

Verne continues: "I was the only CPA in the office other than the boss, so I was a natural to get the job. I went out to this little 20 by 30 foot brick building which was the cafe and the office. Al and Fred sold trucks and parts and did repair work in the back part of the building, which was separated from the cafe by just a counter. We had our first conference over that counter.

"First thing I noticed was the line of trucks waiting for service. Since Fred was the only guy around who could fill their tanks, he couldn't talk much, but he did lay out the company books. They were as neat as several pins. I found out then that Charlotte kept all records and was extremely proud of them. A former schoolteacher who specialized in penmanship and was close to a perfectionist, you know, would keep good, neat books.

Bosselman books were as 'neat as several pins' but no one had time to talk then.

"Everything was done by hand. There was a girl in the office who operated their first machine, a Burroughs totalizer. But the books were Charlotte's, and she let me know about that right away. Usually we make notes and suggestions on the bookkeeping pages. I did that then, and Charlotte went back and recopied all the pages I had marked just so my scribbling would not appear on her books."

By this time, Moseman said, the B-E station was pumping more gasoline annually than any other Standard station in Nebraska. And that went for diesel fuels, too.

Barbara remembers money kept in a cigar box during those years—and "up until we really started growing in the late '60's or early 70's. I guess that was because Dad smoked cigars and the boxes were really handy."

Howard Knuth, a veteran trucker out of Grand Island, had this to say: "I began working for Fred in 1948, and it was great driving a truck in those years. No traffic except in summers. Roads weren't too good but we managed. The best part was working for Fred.

"He treated you fair so long as you were fair with him. You had to be a couple of steps ahead of him if you could, but don't ever let him catch you goofing off.

'You always had to be several steps ahead of Fred if you could, but don't ever let him catch you goofing off.'

"Fred was always out there, pumping gas or fixing something. And he played as hard as he worked. He's just great."

Don Fenton started working for Fred in 1958 at the B-E stop. "We worked side by side, fixing tires, pumping gas or adjusting carburetors. One day, I heard Fred shout, 'Get in your truck and follow that guy. He's got my glasses.'

"Seems Fred had put his glasses on the guy's running board so he could put on his welder's mask. The guy drove away with Fred's glasses still there.

"I caught him and got the glasses back. I don't know if that's why Fred kept me on the payroll for all those years, but he sure was grateful that day."

Fred even paid him his regular salary, including overtime, much later when Fenton was hospitalized with a fractured skull, caused by falling off a ladder at his home, he said.

"At my retirement, they said I could have anything I wanted," Don said. "I should have asked for Fred's Cadillac."

Former Nebraska State Senator Elroy Hefner remembers Fred and Maxine for their courteous treatment of a potential competitor.

"I heard they had a new type tile floor in their

restaurant and I was getting into the truck stop business in South Sioux City at the time.

"I called Fred and asked him to see his flooring. He and Maxine couldn't be nicer. They invited us down to be their guests."

Fred generally was the first to be at the station in the morning and the last to leave at night, said Trucker Lyle Kemp. He added:

"He always charged a penny or two more for his gas but he always had good service, plenty of parking, easy approaches, good food and anything else you needed—and if he didn't he'd go get it for you. So it was worth the difference to stop at Fred's."

Trucker: 'Fred may have charged a penny or two more, but he gave good service. And if he didn't have it, he would get it for you.'

When Kemp was operating a small truck fleet back in the 1950's, he issued $50 vouchers for his drivers to use at Bosselman-Eaton. He told Charlotte he would redeem the vouchers with cash as they came in.

Charlotte dutifully returned the cashed vouchers to Kemp but received nothing but promises. This went on for several months as he struggled to keep his young company afloat. Finally Charlotte told Kemp that she was going to send him to jail unless he paid up, "and Charlotte was shouting," Lyle recalls.

Lyle's attorney and Fred interceded, and the vouchers were paid back in short order.

When Fred thought his customers were having a bad time financially and he believed their record for

Lyle Kemp (above) is a Midwest trucker who remains active. He and Dick Arthur, a mechanic, recall early trucking days with the Bosselmans.

Interstate highway construction in Nebraska resulted in many roadside lakes. The Platte riverbed sand was dredged to provide fill for the highway, and pits the dredge left behind rapidly filled with water because of the high water table near the river. Fred had to deal with this difficult construction problem in building his truck stop.

repayment of bills was good, he would extend credit—"probably more often than he should have," Maxine commented.

Bruce Jacobsen, a dairy farmer near Worms, remembers when he couldn't pay his fuel bills monthly. He told Fred and they set up a year-end payment schedule—no penalties. There was never another word said except when, years later, Bruce thanked Fred at a funeral they were both attending. Fred appreciated the fact that Bruce sought him out and thanked him, saying, "people don't do that too much anymore.

"I'm still a soft touch, but not quite as soft as I was in those days," Fred admitted.

~~~

Browne Barr drove for the Gates Rubber Company out of Denver from 1951 through 1956. He would stop at Bosselman-Eaton once or twice a week for several months, and then repeat the schedule maybe six months later.

B-E, according to Barr, was "not like most greasy spoon truck stops in those days. They were class. Everyone worked.

"And every time I came in Fred was behind the cash register. It got to be a kidding game. Then one time I caught him at the pumps, another time he was in the garage fixing something.

"I said, 'Hey Fred, they don't let you handle the money anymore?

"'His response was 'That's only at night. I work all day and count all night.' "

Like a great many former truckers, Barr became a truck stop operator himself in later years, with successful stops in Wiscon-

Fred figured he worked all day and counted all night. The Bosselman stop 'was class,' one trucker said.

sin, Iowa and Colorado.

"I truthfully modeled my places on what Fred had done 10 years earlier, and I've never been sorry. He was ahead of the pack," Browne stated.

~~~

In 1956 one of the most significant events in the transportation history of this country occurred. The interstate highway construction bill, with President Eisenhower's backing, passed Congress just before adjournment. It was a bitterly contested bill, not only from competing transportation modes and other special interests, but even from the states who got into donnybrooks on how and where the money was to be split.

The interstate highway bill, one of the important measures ever passed by Congress, came in 1956.

Truckers were an important force behind the bill, as was the President who had seen the advantages of a national superhighway system in Europe 12 years earlier.

Planning for the huge national system took several years. There was a shortage of engineers, a shortage of concrete, asphalt and steel. High-level disagreements flourished among the bureaucrats.

Part of the funding called for higher taxes on trucks. Even before the bill reached the White House for signing, the Internal Revenue Service began issuing regulations on trucking firms, and, of course, collecting increased taxes.

The $50 billion package calling for 42,000 miles of four-lane highway construction certainly attracted a crowd.

Fred Bosselman was no exception.

He began thinking early, when the first concepts

of the interstate were being discussed. That was back in 1950. Truman— probably others—had the idea then; they just didn't have the muscle to move it through Congress. But now it was here.

The Highway 30 stop couldn't compete when the interstate was built, Fred knew.

Fred knew the Highway 30 location couldn't keep its business if a four-lane thruway were built anywhere but on top of it. And that didn't seem likely. He also knew he had time, before the new highway could be a factor.

His Standard connections would know something, much before the hinterlands. He knew that for certain. So he went to meetings. He listened. He talked to trucker executives about more than doing business with them. Eventually he put it together, through contacts with a dozen sources: the new interstate would pass somewhere south of Grand Island, probably just south of the Platte River, where the subsoil was much more stable than north of the riverbed.

Highway 281 was a simple two-lane road at that time, leading to Doniphan and, with some turns, eventually to Hastings, for sure, but really little else. It was a pastoral scene where it crossed the braided Platte River. Trees, lush undergrowth, swampy land which flooded regularly. Certainly, no one in his right mind would think of putting more than a riverside cabin on that land. No one but Fred, who had a vision.

Bob Geisenhagen, a builder and a friend of Fred's since the late '40's, probably said it best: "Fred's a gambler, but he just doesn't throw the dice. Every move is carefully thought out. And one other thing about him— when he says something you can believe him. If people around Grand Island had Fred's word, they knew it was good."

Geisenhagen did a lot of building for Fred through the years. Fred andBob worked on a cost basis, then Bob added his profit. Fred knew what it was and never questioned it. "He did insist on top quality work and he knew when it wasn't," Bob said.

Quietly, Fred began looking for the right-priced land near where Highway 281 crossed the Platte. He talked to Marvin Lautenschlager, then in real estate sales.

One day in early 1963 Marvin called.

"I've got a 21-acre parcel just north of the Nine-Mile Bridge I think I can get," he reported.

"See what you can do for $250 an acre or less," Fred ordered. "Who owns it?"

"A Mrs. Gutchow. She's a widow. You know, it's mostly hay land now. We should be able to deal with her."

Fred bought the land for $235 an acre, but that was only the start. He knew he would have to put some fill on the land in order to get soil stability. But he had no idea how much until he consulted a few weeks later with John Neidfeldt, owner of the Platte Valley Construction Company of Grand Island. John, a close friend of Fred's, warned him, "I can start pumping sand out of the river, but it's going to take a lot and that's going to take a long time. You better not be in much of a hurry."

The land cost only $235 an acre, but pumping of sand to stabilize the site would cost lots and take time.

Fred never asked John how much it would cost, and John didn't bill Fred for the next year and a half, which is how long it took to lay a seven to 15-foot fill, including stabilizing soil and some asphalt, over most of the property.

"Nobody, but nobody but Fred Bosselman would have the courage to buy river bottom land and pump sand for a year and half in order to build a truck stop where no one was really sure that a highway was going to be built," said Gil Rude, a former Standard account serviceman who now lives in Kearney, Nebraska. Gil knew the commercial real estate field and he still does some consulting for Fred on Pump and Pantry locations.

Jack Beachler, Fred's insurance man, commented: "I told him he was crazy and a lot of other people did, too."

Chapter 8

THEY CALLED HIM GRANDDADDY

It was late. Only the high overhead flood-lights were on at the I-80 and High-way 281 site where the Bosselmans were building their new truck stop. A Caterpillar diesel engine was surging in the background as Fred and Maxine pulled their Oldsmobile into the sand piles dotting, like so many molehills, the newly-leveled ground.

A visit to the truck stop site gets Fred and Maxine stuck--and in the middle of the night.

They saw the single light on the Cat D-8 moving up and down as its operator bladed the sand piles at one far corner of the site. A con-struction shack to their right front, only a dozen or so yards away, was dark. A car, also black with the night, was parked by its door.

"Not too much going on. I'm surprised they're working this late," Fred said to Maxine as he moved the wheel of the Olds to the right to avoid a pile of sand.

Fred and Maxine had dropped in after a party in Grand Island, just to see how the place looked in the moonlight. This project was their life, and they were not about to ignore it.

"Okay. Well, I'm tired. Let's go home," was Maxine's answer. She continued talking but her words were smothered in the blast of the nearby 8-inch dredge's motor kicking in. Pumping sand from the nearby Platte River bed, the dredge worked 24 hours a day on a timed basis. A torrent of sand and water spewed from the pipe's

The dredge worked 24 hours to bring a sand fill to the project. end about 50 yards to their left front. Later, a bulldozer blade would level the pile of wet sand it was leaving.

"We stick around here long enough and we'll be one of those piles," Fred commented as his foot felt for the gas pedal and he prepared to make a circle around the construction shed to return to the highway. But the car went nowhere when he fed it gas. Fred put it in reverse and gave it a little more foot pressure. Still nothing but an increased whine..

"We're hung up," he announced as he opened his door and stepped down. "Jiminy, if I had a shovel this would be easy."

He knelt down and peered under the car's front end. Sure enough, both front axles were trying to scrape off the top of a sand pile. One of the rear wheels was in up to its hub cap, too. We're buried, he thought, as he looked around for help.

He got back in the car and began flashing his headlights. Maybe the dozer operator would come over or he could rouse someone coming down the highway, only a block away.

He heard a car door open, from the dark, silent vehicle parked near the shed. A flashlight began walking their way.

"I'm scooting down," Maxine said, as she scrunched to the car's floor, trying to make herself as invisible as possible. "Honk your horn, Fred," she said as she moved.

Fred leaned on his horn, and then gave it a few more blasts and the flashlight came closer.

"Here now. There's no need for that," came a voice from behind the light. "I'm security."

The flashlight suddenly blinded Fred. "Oh, you're Mr. Bosselman. What are you doing out here at this hour?"

"I was just coming by and I managed to get stuck. My wife and I were at a party, and I thought I..." Fred was nervous and relieved at the same time and he just let the sentence dangle as the flashlight illuminated the interior of the car and Maxine, still hunched over and not showing her face.

"Let's get that machine over here and see if we can get you out," the watchman said. Fred didn't recognize him, but that was fine. He seemed to know what he was doing. The man began waving the flashlight in a come-on movement, beckoning to the bulldozer operator. The D-8's light began moving in their direction.

Fred got back in the car. Maxine was half-sitting up by this time, vastly relieved and emotionally drained. But still with a mischievous sense of humor.

"I'll keep my face hidden. These guys will think you're out here with a girl friend," she told Fred.

"Cut it out, Maxine. I've got enough troubles just getting off this sand pile."

Maxine kept down, however, and the watchman and the bulldozer operator, whom Fred didn't know either, gave the Olds several boosts to clear the sand piles. Fred was loose. He could get the Olds back on the highway and get out of there.

"Good luck to you and your friend," the security man said as he was leaving.

Maxine liked a joke on Fred every now and then. Tonight was opportunity.

"It's my wife," Fred said, wondering how far he should go to kill Maxine's little gag. Then he decided he wouldn't.

"See ya, and thanks," he said as he gunned the Olds, left the site in a cloud of sand and turned back to town on the highway.

Fred and Maxine had several laughs about what those two said to each other afterwards. Fred said, "I know there are at least two people out there who would have something to say about my adventures. As a matter of fact, I feel a little guilty whenever I'm in a strange crowd. I figure one of them is out there and telling stories."

John Neidfeldt, owner of the Platte Valley Construction Company, didn't send Fred a bill for his dredge and fill work, but Fred knew something was coming, sooner or later. He figured he'd better get financial backing or an extended line of credit by the end of the year. And he knew he had to have engineer-architect plans in hand to ask for backing. Fred had his detailed plans in his mind for years before he ever saw an architect. He knew construction: Everything was placed, including scales, a truck wash, repair-maintenance shop, a restaurant and a combination headquarters, cashier and shopping building.

An architect-engineer sign off was needed if financing on the new site was necessary. And it was.

Gasoline pumps for the cars and lighter trucks were located between the restaurant and the cashier-shopper buildings. Diesel fuel stations for the 18-wheelers were planned near open parking areas of the sprawling facility. Upstairs in the headquarters building were showers and sleeping rooms, including a relaxation lounge.

Fred's plans were precise and detailed and the architect he selected to formalize them, Frank McNett of Omaha, knew he was in the hands of a knowledgeable client when he examined what Fred had done.

"I figured the only reason I was there was to formalize what he had already done," McNett said.

Extensive touring of other truck stops in the Midwest and East was arranged before plans were finalized.

Not completely true, Fred said. He, the architect, and Ralph Dunn, a truck line account manager out of Chicago, and Bill Moon, Standard of Indiana's specialist in truck stops, toured more than a dozen Midwest and East Coast truck stops before they really finalized their plans for I-80.

The oil company encouraged its leased operators and station owners such as Fred to set up service on the interstate system as rapidly as possible. Bill Moon's job at the time was to convince Standard's lessees and customers to move. It wasn't easy, but he had no difficulties with Fred, who was several miles ahead.

Fred talked about his plan to move to the interstate for a year or more before he actually bought property. One of his first approaches was to Al Eaton, his partner at the Highway 30 stop. Fred wanted Al and Charlotte to move with him. They agonized for months before saying, "Thanks, but no thanks."

"We had a good thing going on Highway 30, and we were at the stage in life where we didn't need new challenges. Besides, deep down, we probably felt Fred was pushing his luck in taking on something that big," Al said.

In 1964, Fred sold his third of Bosselman-Eaton to Al and Charlotte, who also bought out Charles' share later. The Eatons ran B-E, always a popular, money-making location, until 1973, when they retired and sold the property back to Fred.

"The family has always had buying and selling

going on," Fred explained. "It started back on the farm with handshakes and it's never changed. We just add up what we've got into something, and that's the going price."

That wasn't the case, however, when Fred began dealing with the financial world in the early 1960's. The Overland National Bank in Grand Island liked Fred's thinking but lacked the loan capacity to handle the project. Fred knew he had to seek deeper pockets outside of Grand Island. Verne Moseman, the accountant, tells this story:

"I had managed to set things up pretty well, I thought. Because I had delivered several good-sized trusts to the Omaha National Bank, I figured they would welcome my bringing Fred into them.

"John Cockle, a trust officer, introduced me to Al Stelling, head of the mortgage loan department. He was busy that day, but asked me to come back with Fred any time.

"We did get back to Stelling a couple of weeks later. Fred brought in the plans and cost estimate sheets. He had everything, including a construction timetable. We sat down with Stelling and Fred said he wanted to build this large gas station on the interstate for a little more than a million bucks—actually it was closer to a million and a half by the time everything was totaled.

It would take more than a million to build the truck stop Fred wanted. The bank choked. A service station normally cost only 50 thousand.

"Stelling nearly bounced off the walls and ceiling. He sputtered and coughed and finally settled down enough to say his bank loaned 50 or so thousand dollars on service stations in what he called 'proved high traffic locations,' but he'd never heard of anything like what Fred was proposing for an isolated spot on a still-to-be-completed highway. The upshot was that he couldn't even bring this to the loan committee because they would laugh him out of the room, and certainly not to the board because they might terminate him.

"I remember his final comment that day: 'They haven't even built the Interstate in Grand Island and you people are asking for the moon. Go back and start over—smaller, this time.' "

'Go back and start over-- smaller this time. '

The bank turn down wasn't Fred's first. Several months earlier he had approached Standard, who had encouraged him to build on the Interstate from the start. They promised to co-sign the note. Fred sent his plans and drawings into Chicago after Omaha and Kansas City offices had approved everything.

"I should have gone myself to make a presentation," Fred said. "I didn't, and, after looking at the plans and projections, they said 'nothing doing'."

Warren Crawford, Standard's manager in Omaha at the time, said "We romanced Fred and led him right up to the altar and then headquarters backed off. We felt horrible. The company's field offices all had approved this.

"It was really one man's decision. William Moore, then Standard of Indiana's president, vetoed everything we had done and worked on over the past two years. He never told us why, but I suspect it was a case of too much money to be spent in the hinterlands."

Refusals by the money men to see Fred's dream

Banks finally caught the vision and approved the loan, but open billing by contractors saved the dream.

didn't stop the man from Worms.

He scaled down some buildings, eliminated a few extras and kept resubmitting plans to Stelling, who, by this time, was catching the vision. It was after the plane trip to the east that Al took Fred's plans to the bank board and got them approved. The Overland Bank helped. Standard finally blessed the project, but still advanced no money.

What really clinched the deal, according to Moseman, was the credit line, open billing the contractors offered Fred. They kept going while Fred was trying to find money. And they didn't bill him until he had financing.

Jerry Niedfeldt, a nephew of John Neidfeldt, carries on the Platte Valley Construction Company today. He joined John and the company in 1954 and remembers well the difficulties with the I-80 site and landfill assignment of Platte Valley.

"It was a good-sized job, mainly because no one had ever done something like that before. We pumped sand from the Platte River bed, the same as the contractors who built the interstate were doing. But we only had an 8-inch dredge, so it was slow.

"The good part was we didn't have to have government permits or anything to get the sand. If you tried to do what we did today, you'd never get done with red tape and environmental agency approvals."

Niedfeldt says that while the concept and product of Fred's thinking "is easy to see now, it was an ambitious and risky venture then. But I don't think there's a

Land for the new truck stop proved difficult. Stability and flood protection required fill ranging up to 8 feet, and even then the buried fuel tanks had to have concrete ballast or they would pop up out of the ground when empty. This photo shows steel erection on the warehouse/office building.

In May, 1968, the Bosselman Truck Stop had been operating just over three years. The parking lot was crowded with rigs from all over the country, and motorists and local residents found out the food and service were good.

problem big enough to make Fred back off. He put that truck stop together on his own."

Most people who know Fred well, recognize that he's a first class promoter, too. While he was building the Bosselman Truck Stop, as it was known unofficially, he was calling on truck lines all over the country and selling Grand Island as a central refueling stop. He had to. Even when the truck stop was open, the interstate wasn't.

In those days such a huge truck stop was a risky venture, but Fred 'never backed off any problem. '

Westbound traffic would have to leave it at York, and later, Giltner, 15 miles east of Grand Island. All traffic would come west through town on Highways 34, 30 and 281 to get back on I-80 and travel as far as Gothenburg, 120 miles to the west. There they could get back on U. S. 30 to continue through North Platte. Eastbound travelers had it even worse. They had to leave the interstate at Fred's new place and hopscotch around Central Nebraska for several hours and more miles before getting back on the superhighway eastbound.

Early construction difficulties centered on the unstable, low-lying ground. Not only was Platte River sand needed in large amounts, but also dirt had to be placed on top of the sand to give it some stability and, most importantly, flood protection. The truck plaza asphalt surface averages 10 feet higher than the surrounding land.

The contractor, Claussen Construction Company, had to plant the holding fuel tanks with concrete, otherwise they would pop up out of the sand when they were emptied.

Claussen Construction also built the first buildings—a service center and a restaurant, with overhead protection and gasoline pumps between them, plus shops for truck supplies and maintenance. The restaurant wouldn't open for several weeks, but January 22, 1965 was the first day of pumping gas and diesel fuel. Fred knew the place wasn't ready, but he had to start round-the- clock service before too many others got into the act. He saw all that truck traffic passing by, and he hurried.

The World-Herald's roving reporter, Tom Allan, wrote, "This week (Feb. 6, 1965) workmen were rushing completion on the upstairs section of the truck terminal building where truck jockeys will be able to rest in a plush lounge and bed down in the 15 luxury rooms.

"Downstairs, their giant trailer trucks can be serviced in an 84-foot long shop which has two 75-foot-long truck pits. Adjacent are the latest in tire shops, a coin-operated truck scale, another spacious shop for automobiles, utility room, offices, barber shop, rest rooms, dry ice station, a large customer-service area and Fred's walnut-paneled office....The entire oasis is almost self-sufficient, with its own water and sewage system.

Starting early, Bosselman didn't skimp. It was first class all the way except for Fred's empty office.

"Shouting above the roar of trucks already rolling in, Fred said: 'We didn't skimp on a thing. We went first class all the way.' "

The only thing wrong with that picture, Fred now says, is that he didn't get to spend any time in that walnut-paneled office.

"I thought I worked at Bosselman-Eaton. You should have seen me at the I-80 place. For two weeks, I never changed the bib overalls I started with."

Geisenhagen recalls that Fred wanted parking

Super truck stop . . . Fronted by lake.

Doniphan Stop 'Second Best in USA'—

Royal Welcome Planned for Interstate Truckers

By Tom Allan
World-Herald Staff Member

Grand Island, Neb.—A man-made oasis, p u m p e d from the bottom of a channel of the Platte River, may well be one of the most modern and s u m p t u o u s truck stops in the nation.

It's the Bosselman Truck Plaza, a half-million-dollar enterprise owned and operated by Fred H. Bosselman just a whisk off the Doniphan Interstate interchange eight miles south of here.

Fred, a Hall County farm boy, opened his new project for round-the-clock operations January 22.

"I used the key to open the new office and t h e n threw it away," he said.

Walking around the eight acres of blacktop on the 20 acres of fill pumped from a near-by c h a n n e l of the Platte, he boasted:

"An agent who insures truck stops told me this was actually the second best in the USA. He said the best was at Doswell, Va."

Fred's oasis is a tourist stop as well as a truck terminal. Part of the man-made acreage has been reserved as a future motel site. He a l r e a d y has had some feelers from national chains.

The complex, designed by Omaha architect Frank McNett and b u i l t by John Claussen and Sons of Grand

—World-Herald Photos.
Bosselman . . . Big cigars.

Island, is not f u l l y completed.

This week workmen were rushing completion on the upstairs section of the truck

terminal b u i l d i n g where truck jockeys will be able to rest in a plush lounge and bed down in the 15 luxury rooms.

Downstairs, t h e i r giant trailer trucks can be serviced in an 84-foot-long shop which has two 75-foot-long truck pits. Adjacent are the latest in tire shops, a coin operated truck scale, another spacious shop for automobiles, utility room, offices, b a r b e r shop, rest rooms, dry ice station, a large customer-service area and Fred's walnut-paneled office.

Fred's only concession to executive status is smoking big cigars. He wears overalls like his boys and takes his turn serving trucks and cars at the 41 fuel outlet stations.

The s m a l l e r building houses a coffee shop and a carpeted restaurant, scheduled for opening next week. There's also a gift shop and lounge area.

They will be operated by Mr. and Mrs. Ernie Kuencel, formerly the longtime operators of the popular Lincoln Manor Hotel coffee shop at Central City.

The entire oasis is almost self-sufficient, with its own water and sewage system.

Shouting above the roar of trucks already rolling in, Fred said:

"We didn't skimp on a thing. We went first class all the way."

Mrs. Kuencel added:

"If they want to relax and fish a while, they can. If they catch their own fish we'll be glad to fry them."

The Alda stop, less than 10 miles from the large Bosselman stop at Grand Island, proved a mistake. It was completed just in time for the Arab oil embargo and the sharply-rising gasoline prices which accompanied that event. Bad timing, but also bad location. The Bosselmans tried everything here, and nothing worked. Alda is vacant today.

Girl pump jockeys scurried to help motorists at Bosselmans in the late 1960's. It was an innovative idea which attracted a lot of attention, but the work proved a bit too demanding for these youngsters over the long pull. Truckers (below) thought the idea was great. Today, everything is self-service.

The Truck Plaza and restaurant (below) in the 1960's and early 70's, before extensive remodeling of the restaurant in the 1980's. At all Bosselman stops, the food service is from Grandma Max (after Maxine) and is operated by the Bosselman companies. Food operations are not leased out as they were for many years. Restaurant operations at all Grandma Max locations draw well locally.

space for 70 trailer rigs. There probably weren't 70 semi's in the whole state at that time, he added, but Fred was right. Even too low. Within a year he was constructing more truck parking.

Parking for 70 rigs? There weren't 70 truck trailer rigs in all of Nebraska at the time.

And within two years the plaza added a $350 thousand truck garage for more complex repairs and overhauls and expanded the restaurant to seat 230 people. The truck garage was leased to GMC and eventually closed because there just wasn't enough space to take care of larger repair problems as the rigs got larger and more complicated.

The new scale house also presented some unexpected problems. After paying their $5 for the weigh, some truckers thought they could skip the urinals and relieve themselves on the scale building floor. This did not make the scale building more attractive to subsequent users, and a solution to the practice was deemed urgent. The truck stop brass, meaning Fred, was scratching his head when an electrician called Smoky suggested laying fine wire across the concrete floor and hooking it up to the building's power source, reduced in voltage to give only a jolt to those who were wetting the floor. Fred wished he could have seen the first demonstration. Needless to say, there were no further sanitary slips in the scale building.

But growth problems are the nicest to deal with and Fred and his family were enjoying everything, still working all hours and seven days a week.

Obviously, truckers didn't create the success of the Bosselman Truck Plaza, later to be called the Bosselman Travel Center, all by themselves. Motorists

Motorists and visitors, not only truckers, flocked to the new truck stop to be 'part of the action.'

wanted to be a part of this new scene, too. They drove 100 miles just to have "dinner with the truckers" and they flocked to the new truck stop on the Platte with its little lake nearby and its fascinating all-day, all-night activities. It was magic.

"Good thing, too. If we hadn't made a lot of fans in a hurry, Fred and I both would have slept in the car over the next 20 years," Maxine commented.

By 1968, the truck plaza was billed as the "Midwest's largest and most modern truck and tourist plaza and restaurant." It was pumping an average of 500,000 gallons of fuel a month.

Barbara, 23 years old and married at the time of the opening, was put to work in the office, but she liked to get outside with the action, too. Chuck, at 21, was doing his time in the garage and even little Fred, now 12, had his shot at Chuck's old job—keeping things clean. Mary had married and was raising a family in Schuyler, Nebraska.

Maxine had been relieved from pie-baking duty. She couldn't stay away from the restaurant and the gift shop, however, and her touches were always present.

About this time the Bosselmans made what turned out to be their greatest mistake. They opened a deluxe service station, gift and cheese house at Alda, Nebraska, just 10 miles west of their Grand Island stop. It was on the south side of the interstate, and the Bosselmans thought that this stop would be easier for eastbound traffic. It happened that it was easier—but also easier to pass by when its big truck stop brother, with all its excitement and activity, was only 10 miles further down the road. This was also the time of the Arab embargo fuel shortage, which didn't help the new venture.

So Alda failed, and miserably. Here's how Gene Graves, Barbara's husband and head of Bosselman Pump and Pantries, explains it:

"We tried everything with Alda. After starting as a deluxe tourist and truck stop, we tried making it a gift shop, then a deli, and even a convenience store.

"Now we've just closed the animal and we're taking our lumps."

In the early '60's Fred was introduced to a new organization, the National Association of Truck Stop Operators. He rapidly became involved. By 1967 he was vice-president. He became president in 1968.

It was a job Fred enjoyed, and he worked hard at it. NATSO was always broke in those early years. It had the usual difficulties in finding the right paid help. Fred was there during that struggling period.

Fred was president of the newly formed Truck Stop Operators organization during its difficult years.

"I had to fire our top executive, and I had to finance personally a lot of activities that an organization like the ATA (American Truckers Associations) takes out of their petty cash," he said.

NATSO was heavily involved in politics and lobbying. Frank Newburg, now of Phoenix but then from Wisconsin, said he made 53 trips from Milwaukee to Washington one year when he was legislative chairman of NATSO. He paid for all of the trips himself because NATSO had no money.

When fuel rationing came in the early 1970's, Washington bureaucrats had beautiful times making regulations. Fuel rationing depended on cargoes carried,

Washington bureaucrats wanted to load the truck stop operators with police powers during fuel rationing days. It didn't work.

and the bureaucrats figured that this could best be determined by truck stop operators, since, they knew, all truckers had to stop at these places. So they devised a regulation requiring all truck stop operators to determine what was loaded in the truck and then decide if that truck was eligible to receive fuel. The truck stop operator would have an enforcer who would open every back gate of every truck needing fuel, do an inspection and then make that decision.

Frank and other NATSO members resisted. They pointed out that most truckers have their trailers sealed before departure and that it is a federal offense to break the seal. Besides, they added, wouldn't it be better to have eligible cargoes determined when they were loaded on trucks? And not five or six hundred miles down the road?

"Oh," the bureaucrats responded, "that's a good idea. We didn't know cargoes were sealed. We've had 45 people working on this problem for more than six weeks. Now we'll have to start all over again."

The Newburgs, Frank and Rita, first met the Bosselmans when Fred became NATSO president.

"They took us under their wing and were wonderful to us. We're eternally grateful. We still are the closest of friends," Rita said. "You know, we heard about Fred before. Truckers used to tell us they passed through Grand Island at 2 in the morning and saw Fred behind the cash register. Then they came through again at 11 the next day, and there was Fred, still behind the cash register."

"At least, I know where the action is," Fred interjected when he heard this story.

Truck stoppers generally cooperate with each other. Jack Rentschler, a Sioux Falls operator who used to be a Standard executive, said, "The Bosselmans have been great to us. When they have people out calling on truck lines and shippers they mention our name. Chuck calls me regularly if he has someone coming our way. We do the same for them."

NATSO members trade information freely. And they all know Fred as one of the organization's pioneers.

"It's a real education to go to Fred," said Bill Sapp, a friendly competitor in the Midlands and west. "He's one of the truck stop operators I could ask why he did something and expect a complete and honest answer. The entire Bosselman family sets a high-level tone for our business."

During his term as NATSO president, Fred not only had to fire the executive director, but also the chaplain. Seems a self-proclaimed minister from Canada toured the country with his trailer outfitted as a chapel. Whenever he opened it at a truck stop he had good attendance, and he went around the nation in this manner, getting free fuel from the truck stoppers and declaring himself the NATSO chaplain.

Fred was no shrinking violet; he fired both the NATSO director and also the chaplain during his term as president.

He gradually developed an entourage. Everywhere he and his group went cost him little or nothing. The "official chaplain" of NATSO, of course, attended every national convention.

One year, when Fred was president, the man billed NATSO for air fare for his "family" to attend the annual meeting. Some of the members knew he trucked his followers to the meeting, soliciting and receiving free fuel from NATSO members along the way. They winked at this practice because, well, he was bringing religion to some people (truck drivers) who probably needed it.

But Fred didn't grin and bear it. He told the minister to get lost, and if he ever heard of him again asking NATSO members for free fuel, he would be arrested. A bulletin to the entire membership was going out, Fred said. And it did.

One board member, Fred remembered, asked him, "What kind of a Christian are you?"

Fred responded, "Probably better than you, if you allowed this thing to go on."

Fred and Maxine always had great times at NATSO annual meetings, generally held in the glamour spots of the country. At one meeting in Reno in the early 1970's, Jack Benny was the featured speaker and, as expected, it was a sell out.

Prime rib was on the menu. But because of the crowd overflow, the hotel didn't have *There was* enough prime cuts to take care of the *no prime rib* group. So Frank Newburg, the action *in Reno* man, went to every hotel and motel and restaurant in Reno and Truckee *after* and bought all of their raw prime beefs *NATSO* at their asking prices and delivered *meeting.* them to the NATSO meeting place's kitchen. The evening was a success. There was plenty of prime beef.

The next morning the head chef of the hotel accosted Frank with a knife in his hand. "I've been getting calls all morning. You are the S. O. B. who bought up all

Maxine in costume at a NATSO convention in the 1970's. A good time was had by all, but Fred did have some crisis moments during his time as an officer and director of the national truck stop organization. In 1972-73, Fred (overleaf) received the Outstanding Truck Stop Operator of the Year Award from NATSO.

NATSA Award to Fred Bosselman
For Outstanding Operator of Year

Fred H. Bosselman, president of Bosselman truck plaza in Grand Island and operator of truck stops in Alda and Big Springs plus an interest in one in Des Moines, was named the outstanding truck stop operator of the year in late July at the national convention of National Association of Truck Stop Operators.

The presentation was made in Portland, Oregon. Witnessing Fred receive the plaque was his wife Maxine as well as his daughter Barbara Graves and her husband and his son Freddie and his wife who attended the convention.

It was the James L. Shaeffer Memorial Award which Bosselman received. The award read: "Outstanding truck stop operator of the year, presented to Fred H. Bosselman, 1972-73, in recognition of his good will to the motoring public, to the trucking industry, and to his fellow NATSO truck stop operators."

The annual award is given to a truck stop operator who has devoted at least 5 years' service in the truck stop industry unselfishly and with unquestioned integrity.

Bosselman has operated truck stops since 1948 and has been a member of the national association of truck stop operators since April, 1964. He served as president of that association as well as chairman of the board and is presently an honorary life member who is active in many areas of the Association as well as the entire truck stop industry.

The award was started by James L. Shaeffer of American Oil Company to honor a truck stop operator who is outstanding among his peers and who contributes generously to the elevation of the industry.

Fred H. Bosselman

Nancy and Jim Contryman, owners and operators of a national truck stop restaurant supply firm out of Minneapolis, were one of the first to dub Fred "the Grandaddy of the Truck Stoppers."

the prime cuts in town last night. Now there's not a prime rib cut in Reno. I'm going to have to send a truck to Sacramento to get some, and you're going to pay for it."

~~~

Larry and Kathy Romines have known the Bosselmans for 25 years, when Larry first became a truck stop operator in Morris, Illinois.

"I worked for Standard for several years before I decided to get into the truck stop business. Standard was all in favor and sent me to train at Fred's place. I got to know the whole family in a few days because they all were working out there—and that included their 14-year-old kid," Larry said. Kathy added: "Fred is still like a young man today. He never gives up, and when he speaks, we all listen."

'Fred is still like a young man today; when he speaks, we all listen.'

Nancy and Jim Contryman, owners of a national restaurant supply company in Minneapolis, second that opinion.

"He's the Granddaddy of the truck stop industry," Nancy said. "There are many more heavily-traveled routes in the U. S., but here he is in Grand Island and he's the leader. Always will be."

Fred and Maxine still attend all the how-to meetings NATSO sponsors, the Contrymans said. "They're not like a lot a people in our business who've done well, taken home their chips and then disappeared."

The Bosselmans were a shining beacon during the brief fuel rationing period brought on by the Arab oil embargo in the early 1970's. Friends, even competitors, found ample supplies of whatever fuel they needed in the Bosselman tanks.

Burl Hooker, a Grand Island area land leveler said his firm could not have continued in business if the

Bosselmans had not secured extra fuel. "And that's twice they saved us. Fred gave us more than 30 days to pay for our first fuel bill from him back in 1952."

Bosselman invested a million dollars for his customers during the oil embargo.

"We didn't throw it around, but I think I can say confidently that our customers never suffered from shortages during the Arab embargo," Fred added. Fred laid out more than a million dollars to buy fuel supplies from wherever he could get them, and then sent his transports to pick up the precious cargo.

"Everybody in the Midwest is beholden to Fred for that move," said Harley Shoemaker, a Lincoln truck stop operator. "He made himself a leader through his actions in a crisis time. We still call him if we have any questions. He's the Granddaddy."

Chapter 9

GROWTH BREEDS GROWTH

Cruise down any cross-country interstate or city throughway. One out of every six vehicles will be a truck.

According to the American Trucking Associations, 14.7 percent of all road traffic is made up of commercial vehicles and 8 percent of the total is the larger combination truck or tractor-trailer. It just seems like there are more trucks on the highway because they're more noticeable, the ATA says.

Only 8 per cent of all vehicles on the road today are big trucks. All trucks pay 37 per cent of all highway costs.

These are people doing their daily jobs. There are nearly 1.5 million trucks and drivers on the roads today and more than 7.1 million people working in the industry and relying on a $150 billion annual payroll.

It's often said, sometimes screamed by jammed motorists, that truckers practically own the highways and city streets. Maybe they should. They pay better than 37 percent of the costs of maintaining and building roadways. And they haul more than three-quarters of the total commerce moving across America at this moment.

The Moultrie, Georgia <u>Observer</u> made this editorial observation some years ago:

"Should you raise your son to be a truck driver?

"Most people would probably say 'no.' After

all, a truck driver is a roughneck who only shaves on holidays, isn't he? Anybody who has ever watched an old movie on television knows that. And movies, as you are well aware, are always completely realistic and true to life.

"Well, it's time to expel that myth. The truth is most truckers would have a hard time living up to that image even if they wanted to. For one thing, their wives wouldn't let them—or their bosses either. Truck driving is a responsible job and requires a responsible man, and anyone who doesn't fit that bill has no business being behind the wheel of a truck.

"Trucks cost a lot of money. So do the goods they carry. A trailer truck and a load together can be worth as much as $250 thousand (Editor's note: now $400 thousand) and a driver has to haul that load from one side of the country to the other safely, on time and in good condition. It takes a good man to do it, which is why a truck driver makes the kind of money he does."

Many drivers might well dispute the newspaper's view on good pay. But none would argue on responsibility. Particularly the owner-operators, who have multiplied since the trucking industry was deregulated in 1980.

The Motor Carrier Act of 1980 effectively repealed the 1935 Act which put truckers under national surveillance, establishing standards for carrier dependability and safety. This included single line rate-making and operating authority, all subject to Interstate Commerce Commission approval.

Some observers of the national transportation scene called this system a federally-inspired cartel. No question that the 1935 Act and the Reed-Bulwinkle Act of 1948 preserved rate-making authority within a tidy and non-competitive industry.

Now, with deregulation, there is freedom on where to go and how much to charge. The trucking industry has grown like Topsy. Shippers are considerably better off than they were in 1980. Niche carriers, specialized through product hauled and/or by market served, blossomed under the new, relaxed rules.

Deregulation in trucking industry has done much for shippers and offered opportunities for trucking growth.

Transport experts will be arguing the pro's and con's of trucking deregulation for the next 20 years, but not its immediate effects—rate wars, bankruptcies of old-line firms unprepared for competition and the entry of huge numbers of newcomers. Most of the newcomers are owner-operators, the so-called one-truck Man of the Road.

The number of ton-miles carried has been growing twice as fast as the gross national product in recent years, while the number of trucks on the nation's highways has been declining, thanks to increased productivity. Rates have not changed substantially for the past 15 to 20 years. That really bothers truckers.

After a dramatic increase in the early '80's, independent owner-operator numbers are falling, mostly because of rapidly increasing costs in insurance and other peripheral demands not directly related to operating a truck. Those problems, plus the pressure of highly competitive rates, are now limiting the field.

Total distribution costs today have decreased nearly $100 billion from what they were in 1981.

"I'm not sure we're not committing suicide, just like the airlines," one truck line operator said. "We have way too much capacity available now and not nearly enough demand to haul. The result is everybody loses money."

Not so, replies Roy Chaney, the 72-year-old Nebraska trucker who makes two-week runs to the West Coast from his pickup points in Illinois or Wisconsin. Roy began driving when he was 14, and bought his first truck when he was 33.

Today he owns two semi's, both of them paid for. He leased the Kenworth tractor in 1986. He has an older White in reserve. Roy paid $65,000 for the used Kenworth, considered one of the Cadillacs of trucks, and he paid $15,000 for a trailer a year later. He'll reach a million miles on the Kenworth shortly, admitting that he should get rid of it. Most truckers keep their tractors only two or three years and then trade them because of increasing maintenance costs.

$80,000 for a used tractor-trailer unit and it's running out of miles.

Both trucks have had two major overhauls. They've about reached the end of their road, "Just as I figure I may be there, too," Roy said. "Hey, I know a couple of drivers who are past 78 and still going strong."

Roy is paid 20 to 25 cents a mile. He is on a contract basis and works with a broker, either in Omaha or Minneapolis, for back haul contracts.

"I used to bring back produce, but that doesn't work any more because I'm not refrigerated. The broker does pretty well for me. I'm calling him all the time because I can make money on this job if I have a back haul; if I don't, it's touchy," Roy said.

Roy used to have an assistant driver, but claims he can't afford one any more. Health insurance, workmen's comp and Social Security cost dough, Roy said "and those things are what kills the independent operator."

Roy Chaney--many miles of experience. He reports age doesn't make that much difference in driving ability and believes he can keep up his regular California driving schedule until he is past 75.

Duane Acklie (above) president of Crete Carriers, said his company employs a truck stop coordinator, who handles all relations with truck stops. Tom Pirnie (below) believes driver turnover is one of the biggest problems truck lines face today.

Besides, Roy adds, his wife is about to insist that he stop driving and pay more attention to her, the part-time construction job he still holds and, of course, the farm—probably in about that order, Roy guesses. Before he drove, Roy farmed. He left farming because he could make more driving, and it was more interesting.

Price is not the only deciding point when a driver picks a truck stop. A bad experience often is a big factor in staying away.

Roy believes every owner-driver has favorite spots to stop while on the road. And price isn't the only decision-maker. For example, Roy refuses to stop at cut-rate centers because he had a bad experience with one a few years ago. The station put used oil into his motor and Roy's injectors nearly closed.

Where he stops on his West Coast trips is pretty much habit, Roy says, and it's because of good service, good product fairly priced and a friendly atmosphere.

Independent Operator Lyle Kemp now makes 20 to 25 trips a year to New York, hauling Midwest boxed beef. He agrees that good service is the yardstick all truckers use to decide where they'll stop.

Lyle drives the heavy traffic routes and he has a word or two of advice for motorists negotiating the interstate system these days: "Be frightened. It's a jungle out there."

Gene England, president of England Truck Lines of Salt Lake City, runs more than 1,300 rigs nationwide. His dispatchers make their driver routes carefully to "maximize unit profitability. That means they're told where to stop and how much to spend," Gene said.

Truck lines have trouble keeping drivers, so they don't like to dictate on where to stop unless it becomes absolutely necessary

Since England began covering the East Coast in 1957, the line has been a steady Bosselman customer. The I-80 stop in Grand Island pumps more fuel for England units than any other in the nation.

"What Bosselman says they'll do, they do. We like that, and what's even better, our drivers like Bosselman stops, too," Gene reports.

Driver loyalty and retention is probably the No. 1 problem with truck lines today, according to Tom Pirnie, president of G. I. Express. He adds: "Most companies recognize they have driver turnover problems, so they will not force their drivers to refuel or stop someplace they don't want to." he said. "Our dispatchers schedule all our driver stops, with lots of consultation with the drivers."

Both England and Pirnie say they receive deals and price offers daily from truck stop operators and combines of operators. They are not easily swayed. It takes more than a tempting reduction of a cent or less a gallon to make them switch refueling stops.

Crete Carriers, one of the two dozen largest truckload lines in the nation, has a truck stop coordinator on its payroll. Crete's president, Duane Acklie, reported that in addition to service and price there are intangibles, such as support for the industry, which influences truckers to stop at certain locations.

"The industry has always appreciated the Bosselmans' help," Ackley stated.

Chuck Bosselman, Fred's son in charge of the

Bosselman stops, is a member of the board of directors of American Best Truck Stops, one of whose goals is to offer combined or comparable quality truck stop services over the country. AMBEST has 130 of the larger stops across the nation; only five of the seven Bosselman stops qualify in size for membership. Chuck declared:

130 larger truck stops have formed AMBEST to standardize service in quality ways.

"We have good shop facilities, particularly in Grand Island, and most of the independents know it. Word of mouth is real important with these guys. We contact the fleet people regularly and have done it for many years. I think we were maybe the first to plan an active sales program for them."

After Fred built the first superstop in Grand Island he built a smaller one, but still patterned after the first, in Big Springs, near the Nebraska-Colorado border. Then, through the 1970's, Bosselman built or bought stops in Elm Creek, Wood River, and Hampton, Nebraska, plus Salina, Kansas.

Fred entered an operating partnership with Moe Hartner, another former Standard field man, for a Des Moines stop back in the 1970's, and then took over the property when Moe died.

The Bosselmans are sticklers for good looks. Even though many of their truck plazas are considered "first generation," they constantly are building or remodeling. Wood River received a $1.5 million complete renovation and face-lift in 1992, and the Des Moines truck island project for the same $1.5 million amount was completed in 1994. "Salina is next," Chuck reported.

Grandma Max's restaurants are the forever- busy parts of the truck stops in Grand Island, Salina, Big

Charlie Bosselman is the first of the third generation to enter the business.

Springs and Des Moines. They were named by Charlie Bosselman, Chuck's son and the first of the third generation Bosselmans in the business.

"He's taken over real well," said Fred, Jr., his uncle. "Until he came along we didn't have anybody in the family who was interested in the food business—except Maxine, of course, who got it all started."

Roger Roepke and his family were running a restaurant in Marysville, Kansas, in 1966 when they heard about "this huge truck stop in Grand Island where they couldn't keep up with the traffic, and the food operation was too much for the older people who were leasing it.

"We went out, saw the place and the crowds—I've never seen anything so busy. We decided we would pass. Nobody could handle that.

"But we came home and thought about it, and it was challenging. My wife and family said 'go' and I went back.

"Fred was behind the cash checkout counter in the truck building. He had a Standard uniform on and was helping pump gas and collect money. We told him we were interested in the food lease. He quickly motioned for us to follow him back to his office.

"We worked out a deal to buy out the present leaseholders, a couple from Central City named Kuenzel. They were really nice people. It just got to be too heavy duty for them."

Roger reported that the restaurant "was a money maker from the start. And Fred was a perfect landlord. He would ask us if we could handle a rent increase before he asked for it. We actually never had a signed lease over

Roger Roepke and his wife, Rosemary, have left the Bosselman food operations and established a small business in a Grand Island shopping mall. "Too many 24-hour shifts," was the way Roger explained it. He and the Bosselmans maintain good relations.

Chuck Bosselman (above) in charge of truck stop operations, and his son, Charlie (below) who runs the restaurants, agree that most of their food business is local, but 90 percent of the fuel business is from truckers. *Photos by Hal Maggiore.*

the 24 years we did business with him."

Too many 24-hour days in the food business, Roger says when he resigned.

Roger also took charge of the Big Springs food operation when it opened in 1969. His mother, father, brother, daughter and son-in-law—in addition to his wife—worked both restaurant locations before Roger determined that the family had had enough of long hours and asked to be released from his contract. That's when Charlie took over with the "Grandma Max" name.

"I just had too many 24-hour days," Roger explainedas his reason for quitting. "Fred is the nicest guy in the world. We never had one argument during all of our years together."

~~~

Chuck and Charlie try to keep the food business at their stops aimed at serving local residents.

"We probably get up to 60 percent of our food business locally, but that varies from stop to stop," Chuck said. Although tourists and passing motorists provide a steady flow, truckers have their special booths, phones and service extras and are always welcomed at the all-you-can-eat buffets Grandma Max features.

Actually, nearly 90 percent of the fuel business at Bosselman plazas is done by truckers. That's because they come in for 100 to 200 gallon fills, and there's always a steady stream.

Harley Shoemaker, a Lincoln truck stop operator since 1968, says business is better today than it was 10 to 15 years ago. Chuck isn't so sure. "Competition is getting rougher and costs keep going up," he said.

The need for supervision is a constant. Every Tuesday Chuck, and his four to seven person group tours, inspects, points to and suggests at one of the Bosselman truck stops. Maybe two, if the day permits. In any event, by the end of a month of Tuesdays, Chuck and his management group have made the rounds. They know what is happening.

In all of his negotiations with truck lines and suppliers, Chuck says, "It helps a lot that my name is Bosselman. If I'm in a special negotiating situation and I need a clincher, I can always call on Dad. Fred can talk t o anyone in the business—and he's known and respected."

Curley Olney of McCook, Nebraska, a former trucker and dealer, recognized the unique Bosselman status early. "Fred helped truckers and their organizations when it was needed—it was that simple," he said.

Fred always helped the truckers and their organizations and he is honored because of it, Olney said.

Chuck said his father "refers most of the truck inquiries my way now, but there were times in the past, much less now, when he checked up on how I had handled the situation."

Sam Gill and his wife Leona, of Big Springs, are also longtime associates of the Bosselmans. Five years after Grand Island, the second truck stop was ready to open and Sam and Leona were ready to go to work. Leona was the cashier. Sam was a mechanic in the garage. Roger Roepke had the restaurant. Big Springs was the western terminus of Interstate 80 when the truck stop opened.

A succession of managers followed, none of whom "worked out well," Fred said. Finally Sam and Leona got

Sam Gill, Big Springs, Nebraska manager, did investigatory work on his next door competitor before blowing the whistle. Sam figured the competitor couldn't be undercutting his price without pulling a shady deal or two. The story broke in a Denver newspaper in 1993 (below).

Caymans move, partner's death spice drama of fraud investigation

Intrigue surrounds Max Oil owner's case

By Don Knox
Rocky Mountain News Staff Writer

Samuel Gill was one of the first to suspect Denver's Max Oil Inc. of running a scam.

The manager of Bosselman's truck stop in Big Springs, Neb., couldn't fathom how a competing Rodeo Pit Stop station, just a gas cap's throw across Interstate 80, could sell its fuel for so much less. So in 1991, he set out on a mission.

"When I was working there, this man would drive by in his car at night," recalls an ex-employee of Rodeo Pit Stop, owned by a Max Oil affiliate. "We thought he was keeping an eye on the prices. But he wasn't. He was looking at the volume sold."

The numbers Gill tracked apparently increased his suspicions. The Max station was selling lots of gasoline, far more than it let on to regulators.

Gill's corporate espionage triggered a nearly two-year investigation that ended in dramatic fashion three weeks ago today when federal and state agents simultaneously raided Max's 28 stations in Colorado, Wyoming and Nebraska, under the names Pit Stop, Rodeo Pit Stop and Mini Stop. They froze several million dollars in company bank accounts, putting 300 employees on the streets. The alleged crime: evasion of nearly $8 million in state and federal fuel taxes from 1989 to 1992, the most in Colorado's history.

Max's status-conscious principal, Thomas W. Quintin Jr., 46, and his wife, Sandra Westphal Quintin, 50, already had problems. Tom Quintin was a federal fugitive, having skipped the country after pleading guilty last year to evading fuel taxes eight years previously in California.

The Quintins, who until recently lived lavishly in a seven-bedroom, eight-bathroom Cherry Hills mansion, didn't return numerous phone calls.

And the drama still is being played out. Regulators and law enforcers aren't sure they've uncovered all the possible wrongdoing at Max Oil and its six affiliates. Gossipy tidbits such as foreign crime groups' participation in these types of fuel-tax schemes and the apparently unrelated murder last year of Quintin's California

A two-year investigation ended dramatically three weeks ago when federal and state agents simultaneously raided Max Oil Co.'s 28 stations in Colorado, Wyoming and Nebraska.

See **MAX** on **32A**

Gene Graves looks over the stock in a Grand Island Pump and Pantry store. Below is the first P&P location, 5th and Sycamore, in Grand Island. The station does not carry the Pump and Pantry name any more because it cannot conform to the P&P master plan in merchandise stocking or display. *Photo by Hal Maggiore.*

the job as a joint venture. "I guess there wasn't anybody else around that day," Sam suggested.

During the 20 years they've run Big Springs it has shown profits. Not always easily, though.

The Quintins forgot to pay taxes on diesel fuel they purchased for re-sale; They are now U. S. fugitives.

Across the interchange's access road was another truck stop, owned by a couple named Tom and Sandra Quintin under the name of Max Oil, Inc. and Pit Stops of America. They were forever posting lower fuel prices than Bosselmans and no one could figure out how.

"Our margins were down to nothing and we were still getting beat," Sam said. "We were losing money and that really bothered us."

Sam began taking notes on the volume sold by his neighbor. They confirmed his thoughts that the station was selling far more fuel than it was reporting.

And it all ended when the Nebraska State Department of Revenue issued a summons to the Quintins for failure to pay back fuel taxes. The total amount involved in the Quintins' Nebraska caper of cheating the state's taxpayers was $2.1 million. Colorado and the federal government were taken for much more.

It seems the Quintins had not been paying the 44.6 cents per gallon diesel fuel tax. When diesel fuel is used on a farm or ranch, this tax need not be paid. Only when the diesel fuel purchaser uses or resells the fuel for use in over-the-road vehicles is tax payment required.

The Quintins, from their home in the Cayman Islands south of Cuba, simply declared they were using the diesel fuel in agriculture. And for as long as the scam went on—better than two years—this certainly allowed

The Quintins could sell diesel fuel 40 cents cheaper and still make a profit.. Sam wanted to know how.

the Quintins to cut fuel prices and to personally pocket significant money. It will not save them from jail, however. They are now international fugitives.

Total Petroleum, a big wholesaler and refiner, has since taken over Quintins' property."They are legitimate competitors and good people," Sam said.

"Looking back a few years, I'm just thankful I was smart enough back then to go to work for Fred," he added.

~~~

The Bosselman Pump and Pantry stores were started in 1971, almost as an accident.

Clem Lempke ran a Standard station on 5th and Sycamore, on the north side of downtown Grand Island. He had a lessee by the name of Lou McKenzie, who came up with the name of Pump and Pantry for his store.

Fred bought the station with the funny name then. In fact, he bought out Clem Lempke twice. The first time was in 1962, as Clem recalls it:

"Fred sees me one day and says he wants me to go to work for him.

" 'Doing what?' " I ask.

" 'Driving a truck.' "

" 'You don't even have a truck.' "

" 'How about yours?' "

" 'You don't own it.' " I reply.

" 'Yes I do. I just bought it from Standard.' "

"That's when I first found out that Fred had been appointed jobber for the entire Grand Island area. He had been handling it before, but only for his own place.

Now he had my station, and I was working for him. He had all my farm and commercial routes, too."

Clem continues: "Now don't get me wrong. I like Fred and his family and, really, they're one of the most considerate competitors anyone could have had. But I saw no reason to stick around after this, so within a year I was banging at the door of the local Skelly Oil distributor.

"His name was Milne, and he said he didn't want to sell then, but in three years, when he was 65, he might consider it. Then he thought a bit.

" 'You know,' " he said, " ' I'd better be thinking about selling today, because I might not find a buyer a couple of years from now.' "

"I asked how much he wanted. He said 'Oh, not much, maybe 12 thousand. If you want to inventory, we'll inventory.' I didn't say anything, but went to find my banker. It took a few days to get the papers in order and when I next saw Milne he announced he had completed the inventory and the business would cost me $23,553.

"I argued. I pleaded. I couldn't get him to budge. I finally even offered him $23,000 on the nose, just to get something started. You'd think he would have halved the difference. But he never let that $553 go."

Clem admitted he learned a lesson. "When somebody offers you something without thinking or getting his numbers together, it's generally wise to take it immediately. I could have had that business for 12 thousand dollars."

The Skelly jobbership was good for Clem until the middle 70's, when Fred again took over his jobber services and petroleum stations. Fred purchased the Skelly stations in Aurora, Central

A casual, first offer often is the best.

Gene Graves organized and expanded the Pump and Pantry convenience stores. He joined the family in the early days.

City, Cairo, Elm Creek and Grand Island. In due course, they all became Pump and Pantries.

There are now 36 Pump and Pantry locations in rural Nebraska. They have a remarkable sameness about them, and that's by design, said Gene Graves, chief executive of the Pump and Pantries and son-in-law of Fred.

Gene, a high school teacher and coach who married Barbara in 1963 and went on to get his masters degree in psychological counseling, joined Bosselmans as a hired hand in 1975. He had been filling in by driving tank trucks and semi's during the fuel shortage and helping set up the early Pump and Pantries. The firm was on its sixth P&P when Gene came to work full-time in the division.

Paul Johnson, now a service station owner in Grand Island, remembers the day well. "We were all working 15 hour days and nights just trying to keep up, and Gene comes in and just pitches in with a 'What can I do attitude'. It was typical Bosselman."

Gene's contribution to the Pump and Pantries was organization and planning, right from the start.

"We try to make every store the same, the same merchandise in the same place, the same cleanliness, the same courteous, may-we-help-you attitude," he said.

"Finding the right people for management is getting more difficult these days," he admitted. "Training also takes a load of time, but it's vital. The Bosselman P&P's run a little larger than the average convenience store—2,600 to 3,000 square feet. The company was lucky to have inherited some larger stores right at the start to give it a success pattern," Gene figured.

Controls are strict. Inventory checks come two times a year and visits, mostly from Gene, are constant. Each store is considered a profit center with its own budget. All but two or three of the newest ones are making money, Gene reported.

Expansion has been steady. "We move when we uncover an opportunity," Graves said. "We've seen too many convenience store groups go right down the tube because they were racing just to get more stores."

Gene leaves his office every day to visit every store and all of his 350 people as often as possible. He knows the territory, he said, and primarily for that reason, will probably confine his geographical expansion efforts to the non-urban portions of Nebraska.

The idea is not to have the most stores, but to have the best-run stores. Each P & P is a profit center.

Bosselman got a start in the convenient store business at just the right time, in Gene's opinion. He doesn't intend to let that advantage over the nationals go by default. Within the next year, all of the Pump and Pantries will be on the main Bosselman computer system. That includes inventory control, although each location is stocked slightly differently according to local needs.

~~~

Fred and Maxine's second son, Fred A. Bosselman, is in charge of the wholesale division. It includes responsibility for purchasing most of the vehicles operated by the company, distribution of petroleum products to everything from airlines to farmers to commercial operators and even to other distributors. It operates a lubrica-

The lube mix plant is one of the better ones in the region; product goes to four Bosselman bulk plants from there.

tion mixing plant at the I-80 property that, according to Fred A., is second to none in the region. Most major oil company lube and petroleum products are mixed by contract and distributed from this plant. Fred also has four bulk plants in surrounding cities.

"I'm the fireman in this outfit," Fred says, grinning.

He's also the frustrated one. Regulations and paper blizzards and changing tax rules, plus mounting environmental concerns, can destroy all sense of reason and order.

"I couldn't do it without some very, very good people," Fred said. "We've had an environmentalist on our payroll for the last four years. We're on call 24 hours."

A couple of years ago a diesel fuel spill at the I-80 location dumped several gallons of fuel into the near-by Platte River. This fired up the local environmentalists. Protests flamed. Bosselman dug up a good portion of the parking lot, cleaned the soil and repaved it. Then they installed a water-oil separator in their sewer line to channel any spilled product into their own sewage plant. Total cost: $300 thousand, and it's one of the few installations of its kind in the country, Fred said.

Fred's product mix helps his division over difficult times. When wholesale agricultural business is bad, the lubrication oils can pick up the slack—and vice versa.

"My son's going to college this year, and I told him to hurry up and get his law degree. We're going to need him soon, and if not in the business, then in Washington. It's getting pretty thick with legalities back there, and that makes it all the worse back here," Fred said.

Barbara and Gene Graves work in adjoining offices, but in different company areas. Fred, Jr. (below) is in the environmental hot seat; "I'm the fireman in this organization," he says. *Hal Maggiore.photos.*

Maxine (above) handles gift purchases and thoroughly enjoys her work; she's there early every morning she's in town. Mary (right) is in charge of buying for the truck stops, which includes a myriad of products ranging from accessories and expensive communications equipment to food and rack products. *Hal Maggiore photos.*

Barbara holds the Bosselman companies together with her operations and paperwork skills; Jan Bosselman, Chuck's wife, and Tracy Schultz, Mary's daughter by her first marriage (below) are busy with the growing computer system. *Hal Maggiore photos.*

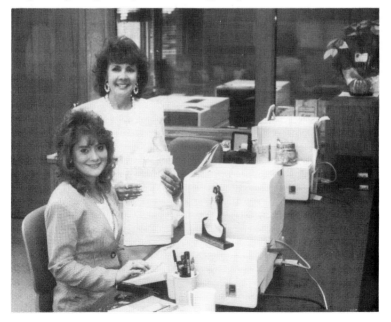

Fred (above, in tractor) does a lot of his own farming. He often spends afternoons on the Worms farm helping Scott Sahling (below) handle the rapidly-growing farm needs.

Stitching all this together— *Barbara is Operations Director, in charge of most of the paperwork of all Bosselman companies.* and without whom the senior Bosselmans wouldn't be able to relax from day-to-day operational demands—is Barbara.

Her title is executive secretary, but she's really operations director. All the paperwork, particularly that involving large purchases and payables, flows over this busy lady's desk. She assigns charges and income to the different corporations owned by the Bosselman family and she directs the flow of business much as a control tower operator at a busy airport.

"I suppose I'm a detail person, but someone has to be," she explains. "Men just don't seem to do this as well as women."

Two other Bosselman women are working in key jobs in the general office building. They are Jan, Chuck's wife, who is in charge of data processing, and Tracy Schultz, Mary's daughter from her first marriage. Tracy is a corporate data processor and works with Jan.

Maxine, of course, spends her days—beginning mostly no later than 9 A.M., and sometimes weekends—in the warehouse from where she buys gift and necessity items for all the stores and travel centers.

Mary also is a buyer for the Bosselman stores. She doesn't have too much to do with gifts, but handles the products lines for the truck stops, Pump and Pantries and tourist centers. Her present husband is Scott Sahling. Mary describes how she met him:

"I had been divorced for several years and it wasn't a pleasant situation what with kid visits and all the problems that go with divorce. But I did go out with some

Scott followed Mary into the ladies' room so he could talk to her. It resulted in a fast marriage.

girl friends a couple of times and I noticed this eager, bright-haired guy standing around.

"I didn't pay too much attention, but one time when I got up to go to the ladies room, he sort of followed me. I walked in and sure enough, in he came right behind me.

" 'What's going on here?' I asked, and he replied that he couldn't get to talk to me when I was with the girls and this was his only chance. He wanted to date me.

"I was flabbergasted. Here this guy is following me into forbidden territory. I had a quick look at him and said to myself, 'Well, if he's this brave, he can't be all bad.'"

Mary and Scott were married within the year. Scott began farming for Fred shortly after. It was another good addition to the family, just as Gene Graves had been.

Gene and Barbara parented two children, Bryan, the elder, and Cindy, now married to Broken Bow Attorney Jim Duncan. Cindy teaches elementary school in Broken Bow.

Bryan, a talented photographer in Grand Island, had his own studio and was just getting started in his professional life when, evidently on the spur of the moment, he took his own life during the winter of 1991.

"He had accumulated some business debt that must have been a struggle for him—he was always in a hurry to grow—and he left us with a lot of unanswered questions," Barbara said.

"I'll never be able to understand why someone with so much talent and so much to live for could leave the world this way."

~~~

With the day-to-day busi-
ness running well through their *Fred and*
children, Fred and Maxine could *Maxine took*
do something they never had time *time to*
for before—enjoy themselves in
travel. A round the world trip came *enjoy*
in 1986, sandwiched between the *themselves*
regular winter stays of a month or *in travel. A*
two in San Diego, and later, in *new twin-*
Arizona.
engine airplane
Fred bought a half-million *was part of*
dollar twin-engine airplane and
flew it around the country. Now *the equipment.*
that he had the time and the means, he delighted in doing
things for others. For any civic venture, or for anything
truckers or truck stop operators needed, Fred would be
available with the time and the air-power.

Jerry Reher, a Bosselman tank wagon man, remembers telling Fred one day that his father was sick in
Houston.

"Why don't you go down and see him?" Fred asked.

"I can't afford that, Fred."

"We'll fly down this weekend. Call him and tell
him you're coming."

Sure enough, Fred flew Jerry to Houston and back
that weekend. No charge.

The former truck driver did most of the flying. He
was always in the left, or first pilot seat. On more
complicated and longer flights, however, he would take
his friend and a fellow pilot, Norm Anderson. Norm
operated an airplane service, sales and training base at
the Grand Island airport, a converted Army Air Force

Shopping in Mexico became an important mission each year for the Bosselmans.

World War II field. He was a professional pilot.

In those days, the Bosselmans probably spent as much time in Mexico as they did in San Diego. They had a mission: to buy all of the Mexican goods they could carry and bring them back to the Midwest to sell in Bosselman truck plazas. Maxine always was a shopper and this was her baby.

One day she sent Fred and Norm, along with Norm Peters, a boyhood friend of Fred's, over the Tijuana border with a truck and a station wagon. They dutifully filled both vehicles and started back. Lunch time came while they were still in Mexico, so Fred and Norm the pilot decided to partake, leaving the other Norman to watch the truck.

When a young Mexican invited him to play baseball in a pick-up game nearby, and another youngster offered to watch the truck for 25 cents, Norm couldn't refuse. He was scooting between first and second base after clubbing a solid double when Fred and Norm returned and noticed the truck was missing. The ball game disappeared about that time, too, Norm recalled.

This was crisis time, Fred thought as he organized a search. That was a rental truck and it was overloaded with Mexican goodies, some of which could be contraband.

It took an hour of making ever-widening circles before they found the truck. It was still weighed down with the load, but the Mexicans driving it claimed it was theirs. Cops arrived. Everyone shouted at the same time. The Mexican police sorted it all out. Finally, Fred got back the truck and headed north. It was getting dark.

"We were missing the necessary papers to re-cross the border with our load, but we figured the earlier cop clearance would do it," Norman said. "It didn't. Fred had to go back to the Mexican lawyer we first used, to get new papers. We got back to San Diego just before dawn. We didn't do that anymore."

Fred had another Mexican adventure a few years later. He and some Grand Island friends invested a few thousand dollars each in a Mexican silver mine. It seemed a good thing at the time, particularly when the price of silver was doing well.

It came time to inspect the property. Fred rented a car in Tombstone, Arizona, with the Mexican crossing scheduled for the next day at Nogales. It was nearly another 100 miles to the mine, which the carload of eager Nebraskans was ready to make, even if they crossed the border at night. Which they did. Which they shouldn't have done, because it was really dark in Mexico that night as they drove down arroyo- rutted roads to the south.

Fred was driving. There were no lights except for those of the rented car. At one particularly narrow crossing of sagebrush, sand and outback, a horse bounded from nowhere, struck the car, shattering the driver's side windshield. Then disappeared. No one was hurt, just shocked.

Killing a horse in Mexico was not considered smart in those days.

Knowing horses, the Nebraskans looked for the injured or dead mustang. They never did find it, but they eyeballed a mess of a car.

"I don't know what the sentence is for killing a Mexican horse, but I'm not about to stick around to find out," Fred announced.

"Let's get out of here," said everybody else.

They drove north the rest of the night, sometimes across country. At one time, a red light came on, but no one had time to pay attention except Fred who silently hoped they could make it to the border before the engine seized from lack of oil.

They made the border, but barely. The car stopped dead 10 miles from Tombstone, thankfully in the Good Old U.S.A. It was dawn. Everyone got out to stop passing cars for help. Three pushes later they got to the car rental place. There was no bargaining. Bills for everything, including an eventual engine replacement, went to Fred. Later, he sent "your share" duebill memos out to his fellow investors. One of these was Bill Hight, a dairy owner who also was a successful restaurant operator.

"I never got into a deal like that before, and I sure don't want to again," he said. The whole group never mentioned the Mexican silver mine after that trip. Nor did they ever get a penny from it.

Jerry Hehnke, even though he's 20 years younger, has been a close friend of Maxine and Fred for longer than he cares to remember. He also remembers the date Fred stopped smoking cigars. It was March 3, 1974.

"I'm going to quit this stuff," Fred announced. He threw Jerry his lighter and tossed his cigars into a nearby wastebasket.

Jerry had the lighter engraved with the date. He offered it to Fred. Fred said he wouldn't ever be needing it. To Jerry's knowledge, Fred has never smoked since.

"Once a guy like Fred makes up his mind, that's it," Jerry explained.

He also remembers Maxine riding a burro to the top of a Central American mountain when she was over 60—and spending the whole day on horseback and the whole next day shopping.

"I don't think I could have done it," he observed.

Jerry remembers one night in Grand Island when he and Fred stopped at the Platte Deutsch, a local club with a large bar, for a "quick one." It was going to be so quick that Jerry left the engine in his pickup running. The truck ran out of gas before they returned.

But some of Jerry's fondest thoughts are of Arizona, where he and Norm Anderson mischievously helped the Bosselmans buy a house in 1979.

"We were with this real estate agent, and he never did know what to make of us. After we finished, he really wasn't sure about Fred and Maxine, either.

"Norm and I would follow this tour of homes trip using a red marker pen and plumb line 'to mark all the walls which weren't straight.' We did a lot of marking. In one instance we told the real estate guy that Fred's car would never fit in the garage. I'm amazed they ever bought a house down there," Jerry said.

He told another story on Fred: "He used to have trouble with ducks getting in his Scottsdale swimming pool. So I got Fred a batch of cutout decoys and an air rifle. And Fred, from his blind behind the lawn chairs, shot the swimming ducks out of his pool, never hurting them but certainly letting them know somebody cared where they were swimming without invitation."

Like shooting ducks in a swimming pool, which he did in Arizona.

Fred, according to Jerry, never admitted he shot ducks on the water, particularly when they were sitting in a line, although he did agree that he probably hit some of the decoys.

~~~

Fred owns considerable amounts of property and

Sound advice according to Bosselman: Don't ever become a bank director. real estate around Grand Island. He picked up most of it by accident....a business friend needed cash and offered some building or land as collateral...a good piece of real estate came on the market...there was a distress sale....Fred always was interested and often got involved.

"I think Fred's biggest problem is that he's too easy a touch," said Tom Baxter, a Grand Island livestock feeder and long-time friend. George Wanitschke, Doniphan banker, agrees. "He's a great guy to do his business locally. He wants to help everyone he can."

When Grand Island's Commercial National Bank was in trouble in the 1980's Fred was a director. He remembered too late the sound advice of his father, given more than 50 years before: Don't ever become a bank director.

"Dad had just been appointed a director of the St. Libory bank when the depression hit," Fred said. "He got bruised, too, just like me. I probably would have been better off if I had listened to him."

Bob Siemers, the cattle feeder, once went to Fred when he lost his $135 thousand dollar bank loan. Fred gave him a signed personal check with the amount still to be filled in and told Bob to go back to the loan callers and negotiate. Bob got it down to $115 thousand, turned over Fred's check with the amount filled in. He has been making semi-annual payments to Fred ever since.

"If it hadn't been for Fred, I wouldn't be here today," Siemers said.

Little things still count a lot with both Bosselmans. They generally go to a funeral or two a week when they're in town. At their fiftieth wedding anniversary in 1992,

Fred Bosselman (right) and Norm Anderson with the new half million dollar plane.

Fred's Now Going 326 MPH

(EDITOR'S NOTE: The following story appeared in the Grand Island Daily Independent and was written by Don Lawson):

A Grand Island man has the distinction of owning one of six of the first new corporate airplanes introduced since the fuel crunch began.

Purchased by Fred Bosselman, owner of the Bosselman Truck Plazas in Nebraska and Iowa, the airplane is also the only one owned by a customer – the others are in the hands of distributors.

The airplane, the Piper Cheyenne, boasts statistics such as dual prop-jet motors, cruising speed of 326 miles per hour and a pressurized cabin which permits flying at altitudes up to 29,000 feet.

Bosselman explained that he first saw the airplane during a visit to the factory in Lock Haven, Pennsylvania, in January where the first model was being tested.

Several months later and after several discussions with Norm Anderson, owner of the Aviation Flying Center in Grand Island, Bosselman made the decision to purchase the airplane.

"When we first looked at the plane in January the price was $536,000 and, when I finally bought it about 30 days ago, the price was up seven percent to $551,825," Bosselman said.

He noted that sales tax on the aircraft totaled $10,000.

Bosselman's distinction as the only customer to own one of the new Cheyennes may not end too soon since the firm that manufactures the motors is on strike.

"I intend to use the airplane strictly in the business," he said. "I'm on the board of a couple of organizations that take us around the United States."

He noted that during the early part of the fuel crunch he used an airplane to fly around the country to locate sources of fuel for his truck stops.

"We make a lot of coast to coast trips and we wanted an aircraft that was fast and that could fly high over the mountains," he said.

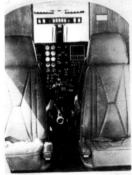

Cheyenne's instrument panel

Before Bosselman and Anderson were able to pick up the airplane at the factory they were required by the factory and the insurance company to take special schooling to learn how to fly it.

"We were sent to a ground school for four and one-half days and we spent a half-day flying," Anderson said.

Anderson noted that, since the motors were jet powered, "the entire systems are different."

Anderson said he will use the aircraft for charters through a lease back agreement with Bosselman. Although Bosselman is licensed to fly the aircraft, Anderson will also serve as a stand-by pilot.

Some of the special equipment in the aircraft includes the pressurized cabin, a new television screen weather radar, air conditioning, an auto-pilot system and an area navigational system which allows the airplane to operate independent of airport homing beacons.

It has a capacity of eight passengers and a maximum take-off weight of 9,000 pounds. The all-weather aircraft is equipped with full de-icing equipment and carries 384 gallons of JP-4 (kerosene) fuel for a cruising distance of 1,500 miles. The two 680-horsepower motors develop a total of 1,360-horsepower.

Bosselman said that he purchased

Piper Aircraft Corporation's new "Cheyenne." It is said to have more useful load-per-pound of airplane weight than any other twin prop jet.

his first airplane when he was a farmer in 1946.

"I paid $2,345 for my first plane and that's just about what a new battery for this plane will cost," he quipped.

The new Cheyenne is the sixth airplane he has owned.

Fred and his wife Maxine have long been active in Motor Carrier Association affairs, and he is on the NMCA board of directors. They operate truck stops at Des Moines, Iowa, Alda and Big Springs in addition to the 2 in Grand Island.

The turbo-powered Cheyenne aircraft Fred bought in 1974 took him far and fast. It seated eight and Fred had it filled on numerous cross country flights. The aircraft was Fred's sixth, and, as he said, "my first cost me $2,345, which is about the cost of a battery for this one."

The old St. Francis Nurses Home was converted into luxury apartments and has remained nearly 100 percent occupied through the years. Conversion was a helpful move for Grand Island which remains short of apartments. The Bosselman-Fonner $100,000 Handicap put the race track into the big time, according to Hugh Miner, chief executive officer of Fonner Park in Grand Island.

they stood for more than four hours greeting all of their 300-plus guests by name.

Art Luebbe, an old family friend from Worms, took sick with cancer during a recent harvest. Fred and his people helped keep the Leubbe farm working until Art could get back.

"That's the kind of person he is. And Maxine's even better," Art said.

They greeted all 300 anniversary guests by name, and they remembered stories about most of them.

The Bosselman family has been in the condominium business for more than a dozen years, ever since St. Francis Hospital relocated to northwest Grand Island and left its school of nursing building in the central part of the city. Bosselman bought the structure, remodeled it and then handled leases. The four-story brick building became 40 luxury apartments, living space urgently needed by the city at that time. Francis Villas has been nearly 100 percent occupied since its start.

Fonner Race Track, a Grand Island institution, also owes something to the Bosselmans. Fred has been a member of the board of directors since 1970. He was named president in 1986 and 1987. During his term, the board began simulcasting races, air-conditioned the clubhouse, built a new access road and expanded the parking lot. A new message board went up on Locust Street and a new public address system was installed. This progressive leadership even built a lake in the infield. The excavated soil from the lake was used to firm up the track. A new trackside safety rail and an expanded turf club also came in Fred's regime.

"One thing we always lacked at Fonner was a headliner race," said Hugh Miner, the track's chief executive. "So I asked Fred, at the end of his term as Fonner president, if Bosselman would sponsor a $100,000 race to help move Fonner into the big time.

"He was shocked, at first. I asked him to think a little more about it and told him about all the promotion that would go along with a sponsorship. Fred began to see the possibilities and he asked me to present the idea to the board of directors of Bosselman, Inc., in reality, his family."

"Never a more impressive board meeting' said Hugh Miner, Fonner Racetrack.

Hugh said he's attended many board meetings in his day, but never one more impressive than the Bosselman family's.

When he finished, Hugh remembers, there was silence—for a long time. A few questions. Then Fred quietly said:

"I think we like your ideas, Hugh, but this group is going to discuss the situation after you leave. We'll let you know our decision. Probably before the end of the day."

That's how the Bosselman-Fonner $100,000-added Handicap became an area-wide celebration time for the track, Central Nebraska and the entire region's horse racing business.

It's been good business for the Bosselmans, too.

Chapter 10

COLORADO VENTURE

Even though the sun was glowing out of a puff cloud sky, Fred could see and feel the chill of winter, not yet ready to scuttle away even when shoved by a brisk April wind..

He looked out of his office window at the I-80 truck stop, slowly counting the 18-wheelers in the parking lot below. There was still some snow on the north side of the weighing scales, he noticed. Tough winter. But then they're always tough in this part of the country.

He silently mouthed the number 64 for his lot count and focused on another group of semi's lined up on the access road, ready to roll out 281 to the interstate.

"We must have had close to 100 overnight," Fred said aloud, addressing no one in particular.

He suddenly realized he was alone and he chuckled, figuring no one else would really care about how many trucks Bosselman, Inc., handled at its Interstate 80 truck stop near Grand Island during a breezy night in April, 1979.

Fred cared. He had opened the office a little after six o'clock, when it was still inky dark. And now, two hours later, he still could hear the diesel engines wailing and grumbling outside as he reviewed the independent accountant's notes on the 1978 Bosselman statement. He was particularly interested in what the ac-

Bosselman's statement bothered Fred, but not for long. Cash reserves outweighed any debt.

countant had to say about company debt.

What was it his mother had said in the 1930's? Never borrow more than you have in the bank? That philosophy would never work in this day and age, Fred realized.

The audit showed Bosselman, Inc., was several hundreds of thousands of dollars in debt and the cash position at year's end was considerably less. Retained earnings still looked good, but that debt's got to come down, he thought.

Fred knew the accountant really wasn't concerned—well, maybe concerned, but certainly not worried. Fred felt the same confidence. The national economy was exploding, with inflation running better than 10 percent. True, interest rates were going through the ceiling. But business was fantastic, and it was growing in double-digit figures, almost monthly.

Bosselman, Inc., had invested heavily in the construction of its new Pump and Pantry convenience centers scattered over Central Nebraska. And Fred was never shy about buying equipment with a loan when he thought the company needed it, either. The other companies Fred had established to diversify ownership had heavy debt loads, too.

Real estate debt was not a bad thing to have during inflationary times, Fred reasoned.

But debt, above all real estate debt, is not a bad thing to have during inflation, Fred thought as he signed a big "F B" on the accountant's papers and tossed them into the out basket on his desk.

Maybe he'd better schedule a meeting later today with Maynard Lif, Fred's longtime office manager. They could go over that accounts receivable file again and try to pick up some dough from tardy payers. Maynard, like Fred, would feel better about the debt situation if the company pressed collections.

A telephone ring at Fred's elbow was a sudden surprise in the silence of the office. It was Bob Geisenhagen, a local contractor and friend of Fred's. He was a key factor in getting Fred a house he and Maxine had wanted very much. A few years ago, Bob finished a gray and white colonial home on Stagecoach Road for Dutch Buettner, a Western Auto sales executive, who never really occupied it. Dutch decided to move back to Kansas City and asked Bob to find a buyer.

Fred and Maxine had just sold their First Street home to a shopping center and savings and loan developer and Bob knew they were looking for a place to live.

The match was made through Giesenhagen, and the Bosselmans were forever his friends. Later, Bob also did much of the construction work on a dozen of the Pump and Pantry stores operated by Fred's company.

"Fred, Jim and I would like to see you today," Bob said after the phone greetings were over. "We got a situation that'll interest you."

Jim was Jim Oliver, also a particular friend of Fred's. He was president of the Commercial National Bank, and mixed with the same crowd in several charity and business groups. In addition, Jim was a knowledgeable, innovative landowner and investor whom Fred respected. He suspected the meeting might have something to do with Colorado ranch land owned by the pair. They had talked to him about it before, hinting he would be a welcome third partner. If so, Fred was ready. They knew him to be a gambler of sorts, particularly when it came to land.

Colorado ranch land was the likely subject of the meeting.

As explained by the pair later that morning, the deal was for $90,000, to be paid up front. Fred would get one-

There was potential in Colorado ranch land capable of producing vegetables and cows.

third interest in a 5,760-acre San Luis Valley ranch near Alamosa, Colorado. He'd also get one-third of the responsibility for a 1.3 million dollar debt on the property.

Fred bought in, mostly on faith. He realized the ranch was not making money, but the potential was there. He realized there was California-size vegetable farming in the valley, despite the short growing season, and he recognized an opportunity for range cattle production, something he was familiar with from his Nebraska Sandhills experiences.

Fred and his brother Norman had rented a mile square section of cattle land near Atkinson back in the early 1940's. They paid less than a buck an acre rent. The owner offered to sell it to them for $11 an acre. But Norman had to leave for the service, and they had let the big opportunity go. That same land went for $15 an acre when Norman returned two years later, then $27, and, finally, in the 1970's, it sold for more than $150 an acre.

Fred and Norman often got into "we should have done it" discussions since that time, and Fred realized in his heart that he wouldn't let another chance at ranch ownership like that pass him by. Maybe the Colorado ranch was an answer.

The three new partners left the next week to inspect the ranch. Fred didn't say much, but, to himself, he admitted he didn't like the way things were being run. He was the only true farmer in the partnership, and he knew what was needed—a strong manager.

Plans, even for the next year, were non-existent. Record-keeping was sloppy. The main effort seemed to be renovation of the ranch house which, Fred learned to his unspoken horror, would cost nearly $100,000.

Most of his suggestions went unanswered. Geisenhagen was a builder and he was involved with ranch house plans and sketches; Oliver was playing the commodities market, and really not paying enough attention to the ranch, in Fred's opinion.

All this came with a ranch manager who must have been one of the most artful dodgers ever. The man was lazy. And incompetent. Ranch work wasn't getting done and no one seemed to care. The guy had to go, all the partners agreed.

Ranch management was lacking; the present one was lazy, incompetent and a thief.

There was another problem with the manager and his family. They liked to use money that wasn't theirs. They sold the ranch's barley crop and collected and cashed the receiving elevator's check, putting the proceeds into their personal accounts. And they said nothing. That cost the ranch several thousand dollars, Fred recalled, and was the compelling reason to dump the manager.

By this time, Giesenhagen and Oliver must have thought their Colorado ranch experiment was reaching for disaster. They had purchased the land back in 1976 for around $200 an acre. It had adequate water, a vital factor in the San Luis Valley, and, at that time, a competent manager. Within the year, however, the manager left. Three years later, after Fred had entered the ownership picture, they were looking for new management again, not really knowing how much they had lost through incompetence and thievery in the interim.

The partners advertised and put out the word over the high plains that they were looking for management. It paid off. They thought they finally had found their management man in, of all places, Grand Island. He was hard-working and had some good ideas on how to make

The partners wanted out when ante-up time came around and there was no cash. Fred took over the ranch himself.

money from land, but no Colorado ranching experience. That didn't seem to matter at the time. He went to Colorado. He took charge.

Everything was back to where it should be, the partners hoped. Everything was in place except adequate cash flow.

Each year the partners needed to come up with more operating capital. At first, this was not a big problem. Then the cash contributions became tougher to come by. Inflation had stopped and money in an agricultural economy was tight everywhere.

It came as no surprise to Fred that his two friends wanted out when 1983's ante-up time came. The ranch was a drain, they said, and there was no relief in sight. They wanted Fred to take over as sole owner and sign for the entire debt.

Fred made the deal, with the help of his friendly banker, and Oliver and Geisenhagen ended up owing him more than 1.5 million dollars for their shares of the debt. But their names were off the deed and they were freed of the ante-up calls..

The first year he and Maxine took over, Fred recalled, the ranch cost the Bosselmans more than a million dollars in cash.

They began spending more time at the ranch. One evening, as Fred, now the sole owner, was leaving, a worker called to him.

"Your guy is stealing from you," he said.

Fred knew he was referring to the ranch manager. "How do you know? What's he stealing?"

"Stick around tonight and see," was the response, and then the hired hand took off running. He obviously was frightened.

Fred and Maxine came out to the ranch in darkness and parked behind a shed. They sneaked inside the shed's blackness and stood, watching, waiting for something to happen.

Around midnight, a tank wagon semi-trailer pulled into the ranch yard and parked near the fertilizer tank. Three men proceeded to fill the trailer from Fred's storage tank. Then they drove off.

Fred and Maxine returned to their motel room and began speculating. 'Who were the men? Where did they go with the trailer?' Fred, with Maxine along, couldn't risk following the truck, but he did get the license number.

The following morning they traced it to their manager who, they found, was farming other nearby land in partnership with a local grain elevator operator.

The ranch manager and his partner were dipping into the fertilizer tank owned by Fred.

It seems the locals were using the ranch's machinery and fertilizer on their land without any notice or payment. Not just once, but on several occasions, Fred discovered when he talked to the hired man later that night.

"Our ranch manager was out of town the next day, so I went into town and stopped at the elevator. I asked to see the manager, introduced myself and told him he owed me a tank load of fertilizer," Fred recounted. "To say the least, he was shocked."

"We were just borrowing it. We'll have it back to you next week," he finally admitted after Fred reported he had been up a good share of the night watching the operation.

"I expect it all to be returned within seven days from right now," Fred said. Sure enough, a full transport

The manager was fired, but then he threatened to kill Fred. The Sheriff stopped this little threat pronto.

load of fertilizer, plus several hundred additional gallons, was back in the ranch tanks by the middle of the following week.

Fred also suspected the midnight rangers got at least three head of his cattle without compensation.

Within four days, Fred fired his ranch manager. It was not a happy occasion. The manager threatened a lawsuit first, and then, when Fred suggested he go right ahead and file, told Fred he was going to kill him. That comment prompted Fred to call the Sheriff. Things quieted considerably.

But these events didn't solve the problem of where to find a replacement. A new manager was needed quickly. The short growing season at the ranch, sometimes limited to little over 60 days, was nearly half over, and harvest time began in August and September.

Jim Oliver came up with an idea. A friend of his knew a young guy, newly married, who worked on a Western Kansas ranch with more than 100 center pivot systems, a large spread in a semi-arid country which had production problems similar to those in the San Luis Valley.

His name was Mark Smith. He'd had a couple of years of college and two more in ranch management, although he'd never had an operation of his own. He might be interested, Oliver reported.

The first step was a visit with Mark on the Kansas ranch. That meeting went well, and Fred was in a hurry. Next, he sent his plane to Kansas to pick up Mark and Wife Darleen, for another interview in Grand Island. Then the three of them went to Colorado together.

"That ranch visit sold me right there," Mark said

later. He could see the challenges, *Mark Smith* and he could see financial benefits. *and family* Most of all, he could see the joy in *took over* running his own show, working for *as ranch* a man who knew cropping and cattle *managers.* and who didn't mind if he took off a *It was a* day or two in off-season to catch up *happy turn* on his beloved hunting or fishing. *of events* There was plenty of both in the *of events* nearby mountains. *for Mark and*

Mark got the job. It didn't *for Fred.* take him long to move the family into the Colorado ranch house.

Darleen quickly finished her college education at Adams State in nearby Alamosa and got a job teaching in the Center, Colorado, school system. The Smiths had two little girls getting ready for school, and Darleen was seven months pregnant with their third child. They liked the ranch home and the valley. In record time, the Smith family had settled in, except for one disturbing thing—the fired ranch manager.

He was not content just to threaten Fred's life; he wanted to intimidate Fred's new manager and his family, too.

The Saguache County Sheriff allowed as how the old manager, a good marksman even when he had a few too many, could be a threat. The man was used to firearms and he was known to use them occasionally for adventures other than hunting. Like the time he shot out the tires on one of Fred's pickups. Another time, he shot through the ranch house ceiling. He had a temper, often out of control when he drank. In other words, the Sheriff said, take him seriously.

The reputation didn't bother Mark so much. It was only when the fired manager called him a couple of nights after Mark had moved his family in. The man said he intended to cause trouble. He'd been drinking.

Mark called the Sheriff. No way were he and Darleen and the kids handling this situation alone.

"Remember," the Sheriff said, talking to Mark at the ranch, "you can't legally shoot him even if he comes walking through the door. He's got to have a deadly weapon in hand to make it OK to take him out."

"How am I going to know what he has in his hand in the middle of the night?" Mark asked.

"The safest thing is to take this can of Mace. Here's another for your wife. You should aim right at his face from about five feet, or closer, then let him have it."

The first night, Mark recalled, he was sitting a few feet from the front door with his can of Mace in hand. And he was feeling foolish.

A can of Mace will not stop a madman, Mark thought, so he got his gun and waited.

If this person comes in, he's going to have to break down the door, and he could be a killer. 'What am I doing with this little can?' Mark asked himself.

He went out to his pickup cab and grabbed his hunting rifle. He felt better. And he remembered the final words of the Sheriff: "If you do have to shoot him, there's one other thing to remember—shoot to kill. You've been threatened, and you don't want to get into a law suit with a survivor."

All this time Fred was trying to reassure Mark that he wasn't in the middle of a Hatfield-McCoy ranch country feud.

Fred told him, "The man threatened me the same way. I told him he wasn't man enough to do the job, and that ended everything. Never heard from him again."

Mark and Darleen relaxed after a week of guard-duty. The fired manager never showed.

~~~

Fred liked the name Meadow Ranch, used by previous owners since the Colorado spread's beginnings. He continued it. He was an active owner, constantly questioning and always with an eye on the payable side of the ledger—something he had learned the hard way in the truck stop business. Within three years Meadow Ranch was making money.

Within three years the ranch had turned the corner and was making money.

It is located 12 miles northeast of Center, Colorado, along County Road 6E. Originally, the 5,760 acres ranged along the east side of the county road 5.5 miles in length and 1.5 miles in width.

In 1993, Fred bought another 4,076 acres east of the road so that Meadow Ranch now is 4 miles wide and 5.5 miles long, a total of 9,836 acres of which nearly 70 percent is pasture or non-cropland.

Mark and Fred run approximately 600 head of cattle on the pastures. They generally go to Fred's feedlot farm in Worms, Nebraska, or to the Baxter or Siemers lots near Grand Island for a 90 to 120 day feedout before slaughter.

The ranch can "easily handle" 1,500 to 1,800 head of range cattle, Mark estimated. In order to prepare for the increasing numbers, he sprayed 2,000 acres of sagebrush in 1993. This will stand idle for a year or two to allow for grass growth, and then will be culti-packed (a minimum tillage process which breaks the ground only slightly while beating surface nutrients into the soil).

Potatoes are the big cash crop at the Meadow Ranch. They're planted just after the wheat, as early as mid-May. The previous year's crop is marketed and shipped at the same time, and truck traffic all over the valley is monumental in the spring.

Potatoes bring gross sales of more than one million annually, but there are heavy costs and high risks.

Meadow Ranch generally sells its potatoes to re-packers, or wholesalers, who, in turn, sell to grocery supply houses or direct to the larger supermarket chains. Prices for the tubers are volatile. Meadow potatoes in the early '90's brought around $40 a ton, or $2 a hundredweight which is basically how they're sold in the field. A couple years earlier, they were up to $8 a hundredweight, or 8 cents a pound on the farm.

Mark and Fred generally plant up to 400 acres of potatoes. This produces, on average, gross sales of more than a million dollars yearly.

And if that sounds like easy money, listen to Mark: "It costs us more than $600 an acre to plant, spray, care for and dig out and store these potatoes. That doesn't include our fixed costs, such as machinery, land, storage buildings and all that.

"Plus the fact that potatoes are prone to blight. There's early blight and late blight—and sometimes I think there's blight on blight. Potatoes have thin skins and pores. When the spuds pass through spores in the soil at planting or harvesting time they're easily infected. This can ruin the harvest, or in many cases, the planting sources for the following year."

Potatoes are their own seeds. Harvested smaller spuds or sliced, larger tubers are used to plant next year's crop. In 1992, Meadow Ranch lost some of its seed crop to blight and had to buy seed spuds at $10 a hundredweight bag. A rough year in planting costs, Fred and Mark agreed, although the harvested crop later that year was so good they ran out of storage space.

The San Luis Valley runs second only to Idaho in production of potatoes. Fred and his fellow Colorado growers realize that Idaho producers establish the market, but they take no joy in their back-bench position.

"We raise everything here as well or better than they do in Idaho. We just don't have the recognition yet. That will come," Fred said.

Meadow Ranch yearly harvests up to 700 acres in barley, 500 in wheat and 150 in oats. In the non-irrigated corners of their 10 center pivot sprinkler systems, Mark plants alfalfa—if he has some way of getting water to the corners. He uses the ranch's two linear irrigation systems to help water the grains.

Surface water irrigation comes from the Rio Grande River, which originates in the nearby San Juan Mountains.

Three or four years ago, Mark and Fred were approached by Japanese interests who owned more than 100,000 acres in the valley. Most of the Japanese land was concentrated in the eastern part of the valley, near the Great Sand Dunes National Monument. But they had this isolated 4,000-plus acres in the west, adjoining the Meadow Ranch. Their 1,700 herd of American Bison was located mostly here. The Japanese wanted 1.5 million dollars for 4,076 acres of potential pasture land, a few wells, a homestead and buildings.

Nobody moved, so the price went down to $1,050,000. Then $800 thousand. Then, the Japanese query: "What will you give?"

"I was in Grand Island one day, and Fred asked me what the land should bring," Mark commented. "I told him not to offer more than 400 to 450 thousand—and if he did, be prepared to write a check."

Fred added: "I called them up and offered 350 thousand. The real estate agent was courteous but I could

The Japanese sold some surplus land to Fred, and nearly doubled his holdings.

tell I had just insulted her, plus an entire nation. "

Fred finally paid $450,000 for the land and all improvements, including a house. It nearly doubled his Colorado holdings.

"We use the new area for pasture. Much of it is too alkaline for cropping," Fred said. "Maybe some day we'll look at a cow-calf operation." Certainly it will allow the Meadow Ranch to build up its range cattle herd and start the food chain from Colorado steers to Fred's Nebraska feedlots.

Baxter and Siemers said they wouldn't be surprised if Fred started his own cattle-hauling truck line to get the critters from Colorado to Nebraska and then built his own packing plant to handle the product.

Fred's comment to that was: "Guess I'll have to put in some meat counters in the Pump and Pantries. I wonder if Grandma Max could cook beef stews? We'd have meat and potatoes for everybody then."

Here's a championship golf course in the middle of a ranch with one of the largest herds of American Bison in the world. And the Japanese did it. In Colorado.

The Japanese presence in the San Luis Valley has gone largely unnoticed since they bought the old Zapata Ranch 10 years ago. They leave most of the land in its sagebrush state. They quietly increase their buffalo count. According to Hisayoshi Ota, owner, they plan to exceed 4,000 head within the next few years. Their most obvious venture is a thriving dude ranch resort with an 18-hole championship-caliber golf course near the old Zapata courtyards. Called the Great Sand Dunes Country Club and Inn, the venture has

Rocky Mountain
Clubs & Resorts

$2.50   Summer 1990

Great Sand Dunes Country Club & Inn

GREAT

SAND

DUNES

COUNTRY

CLUB

& INN

at Colorado's legendary
Zapata Ranch

Large landholders in the San Luis Valley include the Japanese, the West Germans and the Forbes family of magazine fame. The Japanese have an 18-hole championship golf course and a growing herd of buffalo on their 100,000-acre ranch.

Mark Smith, ranch manager, and Fred look over potato planting operations at the Meadow Ranch. Smaller or cut-up spuds are their own seeds, and they have to be treated with care because of the many infection dangers.

attracted national attention. It has a unique combination of dude ranch and challenging 18-hole golf course, including all the modern accouterments and facilities. The ranch has an exercise room, swimming pool, Jacuzzi, lounge and excellent restaurant featuring buffalo meat—and also one of the few herds of bison on the continent.

A Manhattan architect is in charge. Hisa says he'll never go back.

The Japanese, ironically, will be developing the largest herd of American Bison in the world at the Zapata Ranch.

Even the owner is different. Call him Hisa and talk architectural planning. He spent 10 years in Manhattan as an architect before coming "to the most beautiful land in the world," as he describes the valley. "I'll never go back," he adds.

There are other national and international interests in the San Luis Valley. The West Germans have a smaller spread south of the Japanese and near the town of Blanca at the eastern entrance to the valley. Before he died, Malcolm Forbes of magazine fame began purchasing large amounts of valley land, also on the eastern side. His family now owns around 250,000 acres, used mostly for hunting and fishing, but also subject to development, valley residents report.

Most of the farming is done on the western side of the valley, where Fred's ranch is located. According to Mark, there's no reason—except for water rights—that farming can't be profitable on the eastern side, too. One thing for sure: it's big business no matter where crops and animals are located in the San Luis Valley.

"We gamble every year, and every year is different. I guess that's why I like it so much," Mark explained.

"One year we put in lettuce, because I just knew we could make a killing on it. Everyone else was.

"We had a gross return of $9,200 on our lettuce that year and it cost us $1,000 an acre to put it in. We had 120 acres. That's a loss of better than $100,000.

"The next year was a real hummer in lettuce. Everyone who planted it made a fortune. Fred and I talked about it, but we decided to stay out that year. And we've stayed out since."

Immigrant labor, nearly all from Mexico via New Mexico, floods the valley during picking time. Mexican pickers are vital for the garden crops. Mark uses Indian labor, also from neighboring New Mexico and Arizona, for his potato harvest.

Mexicans and Indians are available for ranch work during harvesting. Mark pays them the going wage-- and gives them a pair of gloves.

"We have a hard time finding people who will do this kind of work for $4.50 an hour. I don't know what we would do if the Immigration Service were to really clamp down at harvest time," Mark said.

His Indians, Mark said, would "work 12 hours a day forever, if you gave them a pair of gloves and $4.50 an hour."

They don't feel they're exploiting anything. "The labor market is here and we pay the going wage in a legal way," they explain.

Both Mark and Fred feel strongly that the Agriculture Department should stop all farm subsidy programs.

"Get rid of everything. Put farmers and ranchers back in competition and make no exceptions," is their unanimous opinion.

Fred and Maxine get out to the Colorado ranch five or six times a year. They bring out the entire Bosselman

Lettuce pickers consist of whole families who march in a line, bent over, to harvest the crop. More and newer ranch machinery and an investment of millions is necessary today, as Fred and Mark (right) know so well. Potato plant tops are destroyed just before harvest so that more nutrients go into the spud roots. Below, a potato field is "fired" just before harvest.

Truck traffic is heavy during the weeks of potato harvest in the valley. Here the semi's are lining up at the Meadow Ranch to be loaded for the market haul. Potato prices are volatile but can range up to $8 to $10 per hundredweight, or 8 to 10 cents a pound at the ranch..

Minimum till cultivating is practiced in the valley for the wheat, barley, oats and alfalfa easily grown here. The land is also carefully nurtured over periods of years after it is reclaimed from its sagebrush state. Here a culti-pack process of minimum tillage is employed at the Meadow Ranch to prepare a field for planting. Harvesting (overleaf) is most always a happy experience. The grain stands are good and the scenery magnificent in the fertile, but dry San Luis Valley. Irrigation is a must in this high country.

family once a year.

"It's good that all the kids and everybody knows where we came from," Fred said. "Farming in Nebraska and ranching in Colorado aren't that much different. It's all hard work, and each day presents a new challenge. If you get a chance to learn this early in life, you'll never regret it."

He added: "My family likes challenges."

Chapter 11

THE FUTURE IS A FAMILY

If the boss did a little of everything over the years, getting down to the details on most every activity, and if he then spawned a thriving, growing operation, then it would be difficult to let go. Even to his own children.

That's the big problem facing the Bosselmans these days as Fred and Maxine spend more time enjoying what their efforts over the years have produced.

It's a good thing they trained the kids well, family observers agree. And it's even better that the second generation likes what it is doing at Bosselman.

We obviously see family partnership at work here. The principles of Sam Walton, legendary salesman and merchant, are alive and well and thriving in the Bosselman family, too.

Sam, the founder of Wal-Mart, said in his book *Sam Walton, Made in America* , (Doubleday, 1992):

The principles of Sam Walton are alive and well in the Bosselman family today. It's a family partnership that glows.

"..Helen (his wife) and I did the best we could to promote a sense of togetherness in our family, and we made sure our children had a chance to participate in the same sorts of things we did as kids....(We believe) through our combined efforts the kids received your everyday heartland upbringing, based on the same old bedrock values: a belief in the importance of hard work, honesty, neighborliness and thrift."

Sam Walton's eldest never felt deprived, but he didn't get the biggest allowance, either. The work ethic began early.

Rob Walton, the oldest, said:

"We always worked in the stores. I would sweep the floors and carry boxes after school, and even more in the summer. I remember just barely having a driver's license and driving a truckload of merchandise one night up to that Ben Franklin store in Saint Robert (Missouri), which we all knew to be the best Ben Franklin in the world. In those days, we all got an allowance, too., and it was less than some of our friends. I don't know if we particularly felt deprived, but we didn't have a lot of money. Dad was always—frugal is probably a good word for it. But he always let us invest in those stores and I had an investment in that Saint Robert store, so I came out real well on that. It paid for my house and various other—Dad would call them extravagances."

The four children of the Walton family are much like the four Bosselman youngsters. There was a "do-it" approach; a somewhat Spartan upbringing; a results-required schooling and a "friends-to-all" community service attitude. Plus a "we're together in this" feeling in both families. The comparisons are remarkable, worthy of a sociology study on what makes performance-oriented families.

Tom Baxter, the cattle feeder friend, said it well: "Fred and Maxine spent time with their children, basically teaching them about life through their assigned tasks with the Bosselman businesses. The parents did an excellent job.

"And the kids—they're marvelous. Each has his or

This (above) is the Chapman, Nebraska, Pump and Pantry before remodeling; below is the same location after first stage remodeling. The bottom picture shows the present Chapman P&P. With a total of 36 Bosselman convenience stores, there is constant remodeling, rebuilding and updating construction going on.

The Ogallala Pump and Pantry comes with a motel, as do the P&P's in Burwell, Ord and Broken Bow, Nebraska. Fred (below) always stops at the Bosselman locations, no matter where he is going. Sometimes he just chats, but he invariably notices and makes mental notes--even at competing stores, which he almost always visits. Like Sam Walton, Fred tries to learn from competitors. Here he talks with Cozad (Neb.) Manager Gloria Leidal.

her own job to do. They get along well. Because they are so good in their work, Fred and Maxine can take off for months at a time and not be overly concerned about the business."

Bosselman children get high marks from family observers.

Tom characterizes Chuck as "one of the best truck stop operators in this part of the world, if not nationally."

Barb, he says, watches the books closely, is a tough negotiator and is good with paperwork detail, "something that really helps Fred with his biggest weakness. Barb puts it all together."

There would be no Pump and Pantries without Gene Graves, Tom believes. He put those operations into the money-maker columns "in the face of really tough regional and national competition, and he's recognized nationally as an authority on convenience shopping."

Fred Jr., with his personality and knowledge of the wholesale petroleum business, can become, "and, in fact, probably is right now," one of the better operators. "When he sees an opportunity, he goes—a lot like his Old Man," Tom observes.

Mary, while opting out of most of the family's corporations and business dealings during her first marriage, is now back in the flow and is considered an excellent buyer in a highly-competitive field. Her husband Scott works closely and well with Fred on the Worms farm, which is taking increasing amounts of Fred's time and attention.

One example of family solidarity came a few years ago when Mason Robb, a truck dealer then located on the Bosselman I-80 grounds, noticed the family's arrival in several Cadillacs on a Sunday morning.

"They got out of their cars—Fred, Chuck and Fred,

'Fred plays pretty close to the belt, even though it doesn't appear so at the time, and he thinks things out before he moves.'

Jr.—got into the cabs of petroleum transports and drove off, one after the other, evidently going to the Hastings pipeline terminal or to one of their own fuel depots to be ready for the week," he recounted.

A long-time Bosselman family watcher and business friend of Fred's is John Schroeder, president of the Mid-Nebraska Tank and Truck Company of Grand Island. He says:

"The one thing I will keep in my head about Fred is that as I have known him over the years, he has kept a vision in his mind; he's known where he wants to go and has sat down and thought things through before he moves.

"I also think Fred plays things pretty close to the belt, even though it doesn't appear that way at times. But this day and age, that attitude is the key to survival.

"One of the best things he has going for him is a really strong family who knows how to do business."

John's firm, a truck body fabricator, recently took a $300 thousand equipment order from Bosselman Carriers, Inc. The deal was negotiated by Fred, Chuck and Fred Jr., with the two boys leading most of the specification talking on the prototype units.

"I had never built these special units before, and so, in a sense, I would get some valuable 'guinea pig' experience if I got the business, and the boys knew that," John said. "They, of course, had outside bids on the work, but they never used them against me. They wanted to do the business locally, if they could."

There's a lot of heart in that group, too, retired insurance man Jack Beachler recalls. One day he was called into the Bosselman offices to face the entire family.

They told him the companies had received better bids on coverages from a national truck industry insurer, and that his company's policies were no longer needed. There were tears in the eyes of several family members, Jack said, and Barbara came over and kissed him. His old firm later got the business back because Jack kept on the case.

One former employee believes he was let go because he thought he was heard saying, 'There are too many Bosselmans around here.'

Not everybody, of course, is enchanted with the Bosselmans. A few of the older, retired employees don't like the ways of the second generation, in effect saying "Fred would never do it like this." And at least one figures he was let go because he was overheard saying too often, "No way you can get around here without bumping into a Bosselman."

Fred knows and hopes others know that his kids wouldn't necessarily operate the same way as their father. In fact, in many cases he hopes they don't. He appreciates disagreements and different points of view. When he does get complaints from employees, he refers all situations back to the department heads. None of the complainers, he notes, ever talks about unfair treatment from the company.

If a customer complains, Fred is always ready to respond. He will go to bat for anyone he thinks has a beef about treatment or service or product. And so will all family members.

"Nine times out of 10 these things are settled without me getting involved, and that's the way it should be," he declares.

A continuing rumor that Bosselman sets gasoline prices for Central Nebraska and keeps them artificially

It's impossible to set prices in today's petroleum market. There are too many players, even in a limited area market, dealers and jobbers say.

high, is bothersome but 180 degrees untrue, Fred states. So does his competition.

"It's impossible for any of us to set high prices and keep them," said Bob Poland of Grand Island's Poland Oil Company. "Fred's always a little bit above the lowest price, which is generally set by self-service credit card stations. So am I."

On the farm, the petroleum market is set by the local farmers co-op, he said.

Poland said the average customer has no idea "how close we're forced to sell our product." Many times, he added, competitors were "selling gasoline at the pump for $1.06.9 and he was buying it for $1.03. That's a gross markup of less than 4 percent, before all costs."

The three Bosselman brothers have their gripes, too. At a recent family meeting they were overheard discussing the national state of affairs:

Norman: "We grew up in some of the best times this country has ever seen. I would go back in a minute."

Fred: "Our educational system is a mess, and no one's doing anything about it....."

Charles: "And the churches."

Fred: "We're in a swamp."

Norman: "There's no accountability. Freddie, for example, was in the right place at the right time, but you have to add to that the ability to work hard and be honest—stuff that is not present today."

Fred: "There are so many chances to do things .."

Charles: "This generation is throwing it all away. This is a golden age and we're losing it."

The three brothers used to get together often. They mostly talked about the state of the world, but they've been close to each other all of their lives and often did business with each other. Charles (left) the oldest, died in 1993. Norman is at right. Below--Fred meets regularly with Maynard Lif, office manager (standing) and Tom Roeder, in charge of receivables.

The Arizona home of Fred and Maxine. They spend a month or two here every winter. If they're not in residence, the home is available for Bosselman employees and friends.

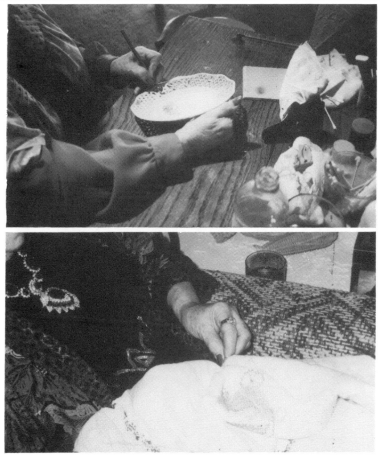

Maxine occupies a lot of her time in Arizona in crafts art--painting
dishes and crocheting. Fred does the area's golf courses. Below, Bob
Larson , a banker from Cairo, Nebraska, and a long-time friend, gives
Fred a pointer on how to get across an Arizona water hole.

Branching out with Quality Service

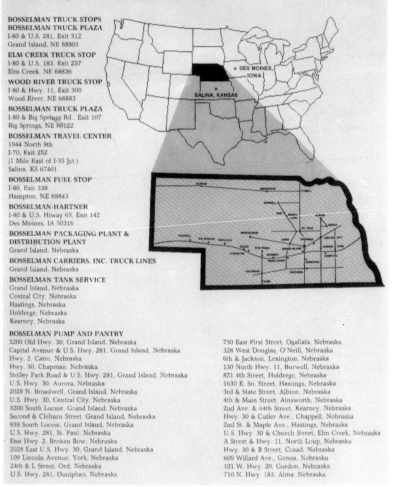

BOSSELMAN TRUCK STOPS
BOSSELMAN TRUCK PLAZA
I-80 & U.S. 281, Exit 312
Grand Island, NE 68801

ELM CREEK TRUCK STOP
I-80 & U.S. 183, Exit 257
Elm Creek, NE 68836

WOOD RIVER TRUCK STOP
I-80 & Hwy. 11, Exit 300
Wood River, NE 68883

BOSSELMAN TRUCK PLAZA
I-80 & Big Springs Rd., Exit 107
Big Springs, NE 69122

BOSSELMAN TRAVEL CENTER
1944 North 9th
I-70, Exit 252
(1 Mile East of I-35 Jct.)
Salina, KS 67401

BOSSELMAN FUEL STOP
I-80, Exit 338
Hampton, NE 68843

BOSSELMAN-HARTNER
I-80 & U.S. Hiway 65, Exit 142
Des Moines, IA 50316

BOSSELMAN PACKAGING PLANT &
DISTRIBUTION PLANT
Grand Island, Nebraska

BOSSELMAN CARRIERS, INC. TRUCK LINES
Grand Island, Nebraska

BOSSELMAN TANK SERVICE
Grand Island, Nebraska
Central City, Nebraska
Hastings, Nebraska
Holdrege, Nebraska
Kearney, Nebraska

BOSSELMAN PUMP AND PANTRY

3200 Old Hwy. 30, Grand Island, Nebraska	730 East First Street, Ogallala, Nebraska
Capital Avenue & U.S. Hwy. 281, Grand Island, Nebraska	328 West Douglas, O'Neill, Nebraska
Hwy. 2, Cairo, Nebraska	6th & Jackson, Lexington, Nebraska
Hwy. 30, Chapman, Nebraska	130 North Hwy. 11, Burwell, Nebraska
Stolley Park Road & U.S. Hwy. 281, Grand Island, Nebraska	821 4th Street, Holdrege, Nebraska
U.S. Hwy. 30, Aurora, Nebraska	1630 E. So. Street, Hastings, Nebraska
2028 N. Broadwell, Grand Island, Nebraska	3rd & State Street, Albion, Nebraska
U.S. Hwy. 30, Central City, Nebraska	4th & Main Street, Ainsworth, Nebraska
3200 South Locust, Grand Island, Nebraska	2nd Ave. & 44th Street, Kearney, Nebraska
Second & Cleburn Street, Grand Island, Nebraska	Hwy. 30 & Cutler Ave., Chappell, Nebraska
939 South Locust, Grand Island, Nebraska	2nd St. & Maple Ave., Hastings, Nebraska
U.S. Hwy. 281, St. Paul, Nebraska	U.S. Hwy. 30 & Church Street, Elm Creek, Nebraska
East Hwy. 2, Broken Bow, Nebraska	A Street & Hwy. 11, North Loup, Nebraska
2028 East U.S. Hwy. 30, Grand Island, Nebraska	Hwy. 30 & B Street, Cozad, Nebraska
109 Lincoln Avenue, York, Nebraska	609 Willard Ave., Genoa, Nebraska
24th & L Street, Ord, Nebraska	101 W. Hwy. 20, Gordon, Nebraska
U.S. Hwy. 281, Doniphan, Nebraska	710 N. Hwy. 183, Alma, Nebraska

Bosselman's growth in service area is reflected in this map and listings of properties and services. A basic Midwest concern, Bosselman has no desire to expand geographically at this time.

The Des Moines truck stop has undergone major remodeling since the Bosselmans took over from the Hartner family. Here a new refueling island is under construction and (below) some basic expansion of the restaurant and plaza sections has started. Fred was a 50% owner of this facility for many years.

The Worms farm and feedlot, part of the original home place, have always been near and dear to Fred. With Scott, he spends considerable time here because he still likes farming. Above are the scales, which Fred claims are a "must" for every farm operation. The feedlots can carry up to 1,000 head and are the most recent addition to the farm.

All of them believe subsidies, including farm subsidies, should end. Taxes should fall on everybody, including food stamp recipients, churches and hospitals.

A tax on "consumption, favoring savers, would help," Fred said. He doesn't mind soaking the rich, either, just so long as incentives to do well are not hurt.

Bill Neuman of Omaha, an old friend, was with Fred when he got his first Social Security check.

Fred was 70 years old. Bill reported:

"He took it out of his pocket and showed it to me, and he said 'this is not one of the top of the line payouts. I was never high salaried enough to get much. Besides, it's all going back to them anyway.'

One of Fred's biggest gripes is the continuing buy-outs of local banks, not only in Grand Island but over the country.

"If we come to doing business by formula—which is often the only way these distant banking centers can handle local problems—this country and small businesses and entrepreneuring start-ups are doomed," he declared.

Local bank buy outs produce business by formula and are bad for regional enterprise, he believes.

A particular thorn to Fred was the buy-out—Fred calls it a "take-over steal"—of the Commercial National Bank of Grand Island in the mid-1980's.

"The Omaha National Bank thought they had us over a barrel, and they did. They didn't buy Commercial National, they stole it. And they were ruthless in collecting loans in a depressed farm economy," Fred stated.

As a director of Commercial National, Fred took personal responsibility for more than one million dollars in suspect loans and the property they represented. Over a period of time the distressed property sold well, Fred

The partners have sold the bulk of the property left to them. Fred's no longer a front bench tiger, as he puts it.

reported, giving credence to his be-lief that Commercial National, if given time, could have worked its way out of farm economy difficulties and remained a viable bank today.

He's in partnership with Jerry Neidfeldt, the contractor, and Ernie Thayer, a Grand Island savings and loan executive. Their holding com-pany, called BNT, has sold off most of the defaulted properties.

"I have no love for all those big banks and I'm not afraid to tell them so," he states.

But Fred, now approaching his late 70's, is no longer a "front bench" tiger, even though he's not sitting that far back. He's turned much of the responsibility for running the Bosselman companies over to the children, and he's turned big chunks of ownership over to them, too.

"A few years ago, if someone had said Fred Bosselman wasn't around, my immediate reaction would be to pack up and get out of town," said George Wanitschke, the banker. "Now it's much better. The kids can take over and not miss a beat."

Board of director meetings—really, family meet-ings—take place every Monday afternoon in the Bosselman, Inc., headquarters building at 3123 West Stolley Park Road on the southwestern edge of Grand Island. There is no formal agenda or leader, although Fred and Maxine serve as chairmen of all six Bosselman companies and often chair the meetings.

Rather the conversation goes around the room, with each family member making a report on the opera-tions they're responsible for and then participating in the discussions. There are progress or lack-of-progress reports and recommendations. All official board actions are voted on, although there's often a consensus.

"We've never had what I would call a fight," Fred said. But he does remember several stiff arguments.

Fred and Maxine call the meetings "the best thing we've ever done. Everybody knows what's going on and we can all keep ourselves up to date."

The one thing that's always done is that no one leaves the board meetings in anger. "We stay as long as it takes to get everything aired. I don't want anyone to leave that room with bad feelings," Fred stated.

Family board meetings are 'the best thing we've ever done. Every one knows what's going on.'

Verne Moseman, the accountant, can't remember a year that any Bosselman company lost money. And Howard Tracy, their attorney, reported the Bosselman companies have never had a major claim or a business-threatening loss or crisis posted against any of the corporations—a substantial record of accomplishment these litigious days in Tracy's opinion.

Maynard Lif, Bosselman office manager, remembers moving from the I-80 office building to the new headquarters building just a few years ago:

"We started here with just two of us. Now there are nearly 40 bookkeeping, records and headquarters staff people here and we're running out of space."

The new building, personally laid out by Fred, contains the computer system designed to keep track of Bosselman's many operations. And the next step? Probably a scanner system to feed daily results from all locations into the master sheets.

No one is figuring on slow-downs in the growth rate of the Pump and Pantries. In fact, four of them, in

Ord, Broken Bow, Ogallala and Burwell, now have motels adjoining, also run by Bosselman.

Des Moines is the latest large expansion. It was originally constructed in the early 1970's by Standard Oil and the Hartner family. Fred helped financially and inspirationally through his encouragement and by sharing his truck stop knowledge with Moe Hartner.

When Moe died in 1992, his wife, Margaret, also a Bosselman family friend, tried to take over. She found early on that she couldn't give the place the time and attention it needed. So she turned to Fred and Chuck. Bosselman bought her interest in 1993. The Bosselmans had begun operating the restaurant under the Grandma Max name nearly a year earlier.

Des Moines has twice-- or more-- the traffic rolling by that Bosselman has in Grand Island, Chuck thinks

Total takeover of Des Moines was delayed six months from the restaurant start in order to get the necessary environmental clearances on the complete package. It's now operating under the name Bosselman-Hartner at the Highway 65 and I-80 interchange northeast of Des Moines and just down the road from the Adventureland Theme Park.

Chuck is high on its potential, saying "we have more than twice the traffic rolling by over there that we have in Grand Island."

And the Bosselmans are not sparing in rebuilding Des Moines. The first of a series of renovations, re-building and modernizing the truck fueling islands, was completed in 1993.

Total staff and operations employment at Bosselman now is roughly 800. Near and dear to Fred's heart is the profit-sharing program, started in 1970 and directed by an outside administrator.

Profit-sharing has been a part of Bosselmans since near the start. It remains an important employee incentive.

A non-contributory fund, it now contains nearly $2 million, and, based on salaries and length of service, is maintained basically as a retirement benefit. There's an annual dinner each early December where retirees are honored.

Maynard Lif, who has worked for the Bosselmans for nearly 30 years, always remembers his early years with the company.

"I had worked for Firestone, where I first met Fred, and for a couple of dairies. Then Fred told me about the I-80 project. It really got me excited, and I decided to go to work for him.

"One prominent businessman told me, 'Why do you want to leave a secure job and go to work in a service station?' I didn't say so, but the primary reason was that I had faith in Fred's new concept."

Fred was a details man in those early days, Maynard recalled. A hands-on operator, he did all the billing, signed all the checks, ordered all the fuel and arranged for the hauling.

Even today Fred never passes by a Bosselman operation. Whenever he goes to Colorado, or Arizona or to any other place over the area, he always stops in whatever Pump and Pantry or truck stop is en route—and some that are not. He often visits competitors. Fred explains: "I have to see what's going on, and the only way I can do that is get out on the road."

Every Saturday after the first of the month, Fred, Chuck, Gene, Fred, Jr., Maynard and Tom Roeder go over the receivables. "Very carefully," says Tom, whose main job is to keep track of them. "Fred's not against throwing 100 thousand into a property and coming back the next day to ask about a $220 outstanding bill somebody has owed us for more than 30 days. He knows how touchy and important receivables are these days."

Probably one of the most important things about Fred, Maynard said, is "you know where you stand with him. He says something if you make a mistake, but he also says something if he likes what you're doing. No games. No guesses."

He's also inclined to blame other people if things don't work out right, said Norm Anderson, Fred's pilot friend, "but he never holds a grudge."

Most of Fred's friends and business associates agree he'll never slow down. Even when he's in Arizona for a couple of months a year, he's continually on the telephone, always checking.

Verne Moseman says that's because he's always looking for a better way to do something. Howard Tracy, his attorney, says he has a unique ability to grasp things and organize, abilities that cannot be taught. "He didn't need a formal education," Howard adds.

Fred is one of the last of the breed. He has a handle on everything. Irreplaceable. But Maxine could handle the business in emergency, the firm's attorney says.

What happens if Fred is incapacitated or dies? Howard replies:

"First, he's irreplaceable. He's the last of his breed— a self-made sole proprietor who understands every phase of the business and can speak to you in amazing detail about what's going on every day, even though he's turned much of the business over to the second generation.

"Second, as extraordinary as this person is, he would not have had the success he did without Maxine. She is a singular type of woman. She never demonstrates her power or authority, but you can tell she has it because she always knows what's going on and she generally has an opinion. She has made the Bosselman family.

"The chairman's job would be handled well by Maxine."

Tracy figures the family will remain in control, at least through the second generation, even though he knows that two out of every three family-owned businesses never make it that far.

"The family has been approached to sell off parts, to 'go public,' so to speak. This won't likely happen because family ownership is working and everybody's getting along," Tracy added.

The man from Worms has just two or three truths he has left for his family and that he now believes may be worthy of passing along. They are similar to Sam Walton's "10 secrets" for running a successful company, but they are simpler.

Fred believes that dedicated, hard work is a cornerstone in any structure. Setting high goals is another. The third leg—and the key to everything—is building a team, or, in many cases, a family-team.

He has seven rules for success in developing that successful team, all drawn from his experiences. They are discussed in detail in the following section. Read on..

Notes

People have asked me to set down some ideas on how to create a successful working family-like team.

I prefer to think of this process as something you can achieve through others; not through manipulation but by choosing and working wisely with those people. To me, this means Success. Theirs and yours.

There are probably few, if any, new ideas here. But if my thoughts bring only a few nods of recognition and a bit of light to your path, then they have served a purpose.

--Fred H. Bosselman

Seven Quality Factors to Look for When You Seek Successful Dealings with Others

...to leave the world a bit better, whether by healthy child, a garden patch or a redeemed social condition; to have played and laughed with enthusiasm and sung with exultation; to know even one life has breathed easier because you have lived-- this is to have succeeded.

Emerson

By Fred Bosselman as told to Wm. F. Arendt

Let me let you in on a secret: I am a poor dirt farmer who struck it lucky. I was at the right place at the right time with the right plan. It worked.

I am what America calls a SUCCESS.

AND IT COULD HAPPEN TO ANY OF YOU.

A word of advice right at the start: There are no secrets, no magic. There are some things you should know and there are some signs to look for. But the path is really straight and clear, now that I have the time to look back.

Anyway, if you've read this far, you're possibly interested in what this lucky senior has to say about... S U C C E S S.

First, it depends on other people.

Second, it depends on how you judge and select those people who will share your work and your life.

And third, it depends on how you plan your life and how you discipline yourself to follow that plan.

I suppose we should define S U C C E S S in what I would call American terms right here and now.

It's not money, although nobody around me is complaining about having too much.

It's all of what Emerson says it is at the start of this piece--and more.

To me, S U C C E S S is a feeling. A feeling, basically, of accomplishment, of having done a good job in whatever you're doing.

I don't have to define that feeling. You all know it. If you don't you haven't lived, and you shouldn't be sitting around reading this book. You should be out doing something, anything, so you, too, sooner or later, can know the feeling of a job well done.

We'll not spend a lot of time on planning and life discipline, the third point you read about a few paragraphs ago. You all have heard many times about the importance of planning.

David Sarnoff, the former TV network chief, may have said it best...."A life that hasn't a definite plan is likely to become driftwood."

So, if we can agree, you may simply need a list of goals, written or always remembered, and a plan on how to get to those goals; one that can be revised as you go through life. What more is to be said on this subject? Not much. So I won't.

Paul Harvey offers a few words on people who speak in few words. He tells the story of New York Judge Howard Dawson who was sitting in his tax courtroom one day listening to this plea:

"As God is my judge, I do not owe this tax."

Judge Dawson replied: "He isn't. I am. You do. Next case."

There's a lot to be said about your relations with other people, however, and how they can become so much a part of your S U C C E S S formula.

Right here I'd like to register a thought that's behind this entire process...No matter how well you work or how great your personality, your family or your purse, or any other quality for that matter, you will never get very far unless you learn to work through others.

By now you're probably wondering why I'm spelling S U C C E S S as I am. It's to emphasize that I believe there are seven steps--or seven QUALITY FACTORS--in all of your dealings with others, just as there are seven letters in the word S U C C E S S.

Perhaps you can remember my seven-point program easier when you associate it with a seven letter word spelling S U C C E S S. I know I can when I talk about it.

Reminds me of some advice for a long and fruitful life given by a lady of 104 years: "Stay away from doctors--and from men!" That has seven words, too. She remembered it a long time.

These seven qualities are what you look for in

others: **7 Q Factors**

in dealings with others:

Steady Work	S
Unified Family	U
Complete Honesty	C
Competent Talent	C
Easy Humor	E
Solid Reputation	S
Specific Ambition	S

If you find these qualities present in your associates--in large amounts--you have found winners. But if you find them present even in small amounts and this person knows how to work, then he or she can be invaluable to you.

Let's talk about the first Quality Factor--**Work**.

There is nothing in this entire list more important than knowing how to work.

Henry Giles, the philosopher, once said:

"Man must work. That is certain as the sun. But he may work grudgingly or he may work gratefully; he may work as a man, or he may work as a machine. There is no work so rude, that he may not exalt it; no work so impassive, that he may breathe a soul into it; no work so dull that he may not enliven it."

We never studied philosophers in my time, but we knew pretty well what they, or better, what our folks, were saying--and they were saying, whether you liked it or not, you're going to work!

In Worms, that's just how it was. We got up at daybreak, or even before, if it was our turn with the chores. After we filled the feed bunkers for the cattle, we took care of the chickens. Then we milked the cows. Then we cleaned the horse stalls. Then we were ready to begin our workday.

There were no complaints. Everybody knew what he had to do. Everybody took his or her turn at bad jobs.

I had three brothers, two of them only a couple of years older than I and one, a half brother (my Dad's first wife died; I never knew her) who was some 15 years older and who was really the big guy we trusted and turned to whenever we got in trouble. He had his own life by then, but he took the time to help us.

We needed it, too, because my Dad was sick and crippled when my brothers and I were teenagers. If we hadn't had a big, caring half brother and a lot of helpful neighbors, we never would have made it on that farm near Worms in the 1930's.

I learned one lesson then, and it has stayed with me a long time: <u>In life, you've got to give more than you take.</u>

Maxine and I, if we're nothing else, we're good workers. We've tried to teach our kids to work hard, too, although I don't think we ever sat them down and told them as much.

We tried to do it by what we call the Watch This Method, without ever saying "watch this." It's a simple matter of training yourself to do only those things you believe might set examples when the kids are around. Maybe it's saying "no" to yourself several times so you get in the habit. From what our friends and neighbors report, the youngsters learned well.

What bothers me most these days, I suppose, is a general attitude shown towards work. It's a downer. It's something that has to be done to reach a time to play. The TGIF (Thank God It's Friday) syndrome is too big to fight; we all let it get that way, so we're all guilty of creating our own monsters--many workers who only wait for Fridays.

I don't mean to say no one should have time to play. But these days the emphasis seems to be on play, not on work.

What does this do to democracy in the long pull? What does this do to the way of life Americans have grown to know and love? Does it put us in a down spiral for all time?

I don't think so. Neither should you.

In truth, adversity actually helps. As a whole, America will do better because we're discovering that we can play as hard--and maybe, even as long--as we work. For those hundreds of us who opt out through laziness, drugs and attitudes, there are hundreds more who are stepping up to more work to create more progress.

I learned this poem a long time ago; in fact, I think it was framed and hung in our offices at one time:

> *Deliver me from all evildoers that talk nothing*
> *but sickness and failure;*
> *Grant me the companionship of men who think success*
> *and men who work for it;*
> *Loan me associates who cheerfully face the problems*
> *of the day and try hard to overcome them;*
> *Relieve me of all cynics and critics.*
> *Give me good health and the strength*
> *to be of real service to the world,*
> *and I'll get all that's good for me,*
> *and will what's left to those who really want it.*

> *--William Feather*

Our second Quality Factor is **Family**, something that should rhyme with work, but doesn't--not because they don't go together. They do!

In my book, a family cannot be a functioning unit unless every member is a worker. That's how we operate in the Bosselman family, and that's how I was brought up.

I have a great fear these days that America is losing strength in the world because we are losing our family structures--marriage, children, homes, church and school. We are losing them to the need for more money.

In a stride by stride process, we now have better than 80 percent of American women working, with the number increasing daily. As a direct result of this, more than half the marriages today end up in divorce. And the final consequence: one of every four American children growing up in the 1990's will eventually enter a stepfamily.

Not a pretty scene, including soaring juvenile crime, teen-age suicides, school violence and shrinking church attendance.

Even the social engineers, the do-gooders of the 1960's who told us "If it feels right, do it," are becoming alarmed.

The <u>Atlantic Monthly</u> in a cover article in April, 1993, said: "After decades of public dispute...evidence from social science research is coming in. The dissolution of two-parent families, though it may benefit the adults involved, is harmful to many children and dramatically undermines our society."

Blame for this state of affairs can be spread far and wide. The media--mostly television and movies--have a heavy role, as do liberal educators who love to teach social awareness courses rather than the three R's. Pop musicians and artists don't help. Mostly, however, we can blame ourselves and our greediness.

Why can't we see the values of the two-parent family, where dads play one role and moms another, and children can feel a sense of stability and permanence?

We'll never return to the days of TV's "Leave It to Beaver" family stories but neither should we, by default, slide into a "Ridicule Your Family Age" which seems to have taken over television these days.

Dad is really not a stumbling bumpkin and Mom is not a shrieking telephone and shopping addict. Brothers and sisters are not always for laughs. I shudder when I watch most TV programs these days. I wonder what messages are being delivered.

It used to be, in my time, that women knew what men seemingly have forgotten--that the top spiritual and economic unit of any civilization is the family. And I think the gals still know it. More money, sometimes survival, just became more important. Who can fault them for that?

Please don't get the idea that I'm against women working. In the workplace, they're some of the best people around. All the women in my family have worked since they were tots. Maxine, now past the three score and 10 years allotted to most of us, still spends most of her days and some of her weekends in the office. As I said earlier, look for the family that's not afraid of work and you have a winner.

For every job above entry level, the Bosselman companies require an interview with the spouse; particularly do I take an interest in managerial applicants and their spouses. I figure both of them, whether they're directly on the payroll or not, are going to be working with us a long time.

So what's the answer? You rightly ask.

You, Fred Bosselman, say women make great workers and you also say they should stay home and take care of their families. You can't have it both ways.

Yes, I believe we can.

I think more and more women are going to see the values of family and devote more time to home. There are signs of that happening even now. A recent public opinion poll showed the attitude of "I'm just a busy housewife (with many reasons/apologies)" going away.

For the last 20 years, for example, about 30% of working women said they would quit their jobs if they didn't need the money. In 1989, that number grew to 38%--and by 1991, it jumped to 56%.

The wish to return to the family is there. Stay-at-home moms are becoming more the "in" thing in our pop culture. That will be a help.

We, as employers, should offer everything we can to encourage fewer office hours and more home hours. Split shifts, part-time, you name it. We can do it and should, without government laws or interference.

Employers also should create a solid, road-to-the-top career path for those women who choose not to stay at home or to have families or to spend much time nesting or nurturing. These women are certainly entitled to compete, and they will win their share of the workplace battles.

I believe that unless we all pay attention, the American family will take some heavy hits before our kids show much improvement.

"The family is responsible for teaching lessons of independence, self-restraint, responsibility and right conduct--all of which are essential to a free, democratic society," is how the Atlantic Monthly puts the problem.

It may take some time, but Americans can beat this rap. In the meantime, encourage and look for those family values in the Quality Factor searches!

Honesty, our third Quality Factor, has been taking some blows recently, too.

It seems our "Get-It-Now" philosophy has given birth to a few shortcuts in the Honor Code. Witness the savings and loan scandals, the Wall Street plundering and the crowded criminal court dockets.

In fact, crime seems to be the only big business in America to escape any government meddling. I've often thought we could stop crime completely if we could put as many cops on the street as there are today on TV.

My business and my life have been constructed on the cornerstone of honesty. If ever there was a necessary ingredient for success it would be "to give honest effort for the dollar."

Obviously, some things in everyone's life are not going to work out well. I've always approached these failures with the thought that if someone in my employ or someone I hired caused it, then they should be told, but never punished if they gave an honest effort.

You've all heard the gag about watching out every

night for the guy who says "he is as honest as the day is long," but I've long been suspicious of anyone who tells me how honest he is. Honesty isn't something you really talk much about. You either have it or you don't, and there's not much to say either way.

Sometimes we ask a question in interviews something like this: "If you knew no one would ever find out, what would you most like to do?"

If the answer comes back "rob a bank" or "steal a million dollars" or something like that then we give that person a little more time and attention in that interview. They didn't give a wrong answer. In fact, if other personality traits bear it out, they could have given a very right answer. We just check them out a bit more carefully. You're going to have to go on "gut" feelings a lot when you're testing for honesty. That's not all bad.

I've found that most "do-ers" in the world today have long antennas when it comes to judging their fellow men and women. They listen. They question. They evaluate based on their experience and then they decide.

Honesty is one of the intangibles they make a judgment on. And they're right much more often than they're wrong. Otherwise they wouldn't be where they are--at the top of the heap.

My point here is that you, too, will have to make judgments on the honesty of individuals with whom you choose to associate if you're going to have S U C C E S S in life.

You'll note I used the plural word, judgments. More than once, you'll do this simply because it will be necessary. No one, even a trusted associate, remains the same all of his or her life. Stresses and changes unknown to you will crop up. So stay alert.

Remember, if you are honest only because you think it is the best policy, your honesty already has been corrupted.

I often put honesty and loyalty together. They are the greatest qualities you can find in another person.

So we come to **talent** in others.

Did you think it would come higher on the list of Quality Factors?

In truth, talent can be dangerous. A beautiful and rare thing, talent generally comes in packages difficult to handle and, in practically all cases I have known, easy to explode. Talent is a wondrous thing to have, and a really big plus if you have it on your side. That's why I rank it so high, even though I don't understand it completely.

I also know that no one ever climbed a hill by just looking at it.

So you take some chances on people; if they're people with talent you'll have an interesting trip up that hill. You generally won't regret it, either.

Many people define talent as creative ability. I think the two are much different. Talent is that God-given skill that enables certain people to accomplish certain things easily and well. Not everything, and likely, not most things. That's a judgment mistake many people make. Just because an individual is talented at a certain task doesn't mean he or she is talented at all things or even offers superior knowledge on matters not related to his or her particular talent.

Creative ability is more a self-motivated drive that springs from curiousity and intuition--the way a person thinks, for example. And it can be present in people with limited talent. It can be self-taught. It's basically a discipline that in my thinking, at least, should be aimed at hitting goals on time with the targeted results.

Steve Allen, the great comedian, writer, musician and story-teller, believes talent comes from a unique blend of circumstances, including living environment and heredity. Add to that dreams, he says. Most talented people, he observes, are somewhat other-worldly. They really take off on their dreams, expecially if it involves a creative solution. *A warning: They're not always right!*

I prefer to think that there's nothing mystical in talent, although I must confess that I am constantly amazed at what some talented people come up with. Maybe that's what makes them so interesting.

There is talent almost everywhere you look today. In my time we were so busy working to keep food on the table we had little time to polish our hobbies or concentrate on just one phase of our lives. That is what a talented person needs--concentration on his or her specialty. If you're fortunate enough to have just one or two of these people around--no matter what they do--give them all the slack rope you can. They may produce wonders.

But talent or creative ability is nothing if it's not used. I remember a short piece by Basil S. Walsh that I've tried to model my life on. It goes something like this:

One big reason men do not develop
greater abilities...
is because they use neither their abilities nor
their opportunities.
We don't need more strength or more ability or
greater opportunity.
What we need is to use what we have.
Men fail and their families suffer deprivations
when all the time these men have in their possession
the same assets other men are using to accumulate
fortunes.
Life doesn't cheat. It doesn't pay in counterfeit coin.
It doesn't lock up shop and go home when pay-day
comes.
It pays every man exactly what he has earned.
The age-old law that a man gets what he earns

hasn't been suspended.
When we take that truth home and believe it,
we've turned a big corner on the high road
that runs straight to success.

I believe, like Andrew Carnegie, that the average guy puts only a quarter of his energy and ability into his work; that the world takes off its hat to those who put in more than 50 percent of their capacity, and stands on its head for those few and far between souls who devote 100 percent.

So it's not talent, but the ability to use it continuously that's important. One last word on talent: Don't overlook those seemingly odd ones when you're putting your Quality Factor team together!

Why do I put **Humor** in this list of Quality Factors you seek in others?

Because a sense of humor can help anyone overlook the ugly things in life, tolerate the unpleasant, cope with the unexpected and maybe, just maybe, smile through the unbearable.

And you think you won't need some help, sooner or later, from humor? That these things won't happen to you? Try again, friend. And this time, smile a little!

I always thought a good definition of humor was spilling the groceries out of the sack you're carrying while you are telling your wife how to handle sacks filled with groceries. Humor is really the other side of tragedy, when you stop to think about it.

Give me the guy or gal who can laugh a little at his or her mistakes; who can find a funny slant in an otherwise serious situation, and I'll guarantee that person is worth having around!

I love slapstick. The Oliver Hardy and Stan Laurel pieces were great. Nobody ever came close to the Three

Stooges in my book.

Birthday cards have become so much fun that I almost look forward to another year. Get well cards can help a lot. If you can laugh, you're not really sick, my mother used to say.

It's true. These days a sense a humor is like the oil in life's engine. I wouldn't have it otherwise.

My older brother, Art, now of Boise, Idaho, tells a story of the early days in Howard County, Nebraska, where the bartender in one of the town's most popular taverns was a stutterer. Some of the local customers, brother Art included, decided one day that it would be a good idea to introduce another person who stuttered to him. They would have had something in common; they might even become friends, Art reasoned.

So the group brought their stutterer into the bar and introduced him to the stuttering bartender.

"I-I-I-I-am-pu-pu-pleased-tu-to-meet-you," said the first stutterer.

"Nu-Nu-Nu-No-you're-not," replied the bartender as he leaped over the bar, punching wildly at the newcomer.

Brother Art said the whole barroom then got into the fight, with everybody swinging at anybody close. Everybody except Art who was quietly drinking at one corner of the bar and wondering what happened to his friendly gesture.

The bartender, when he calmed down and finished picking up the pieces, explained he thought he was being made fun of by the other stutterer. The worst of it was for the do-gooders: Those two fellows eventually became close friends whose conversations together drove non-stutterers wild.

I was close to Art all of my life, even though he was a lot older. He taught me a lot about farming--and about living. He could always manage a laugh, even in those

1930's depression years.

One of the things he said has always stayed with me: "Freddie, you can call yourself a man when you enjoy your first big joke--on yourself."

One of this country's greatest assets is the ability to laugh at ourselves. That sense of humor will carry us through a lot, as it will carry you and your friends and business associates through a lot.

We all have five senses: seeing, hearing, touching, smelling and tasting. I submit we need a sixth--a sense of humor.

My education is lacking; I just got through eighth grade because I was needed on the farm when my Dad took sick. Therefore, while I didn't study a lot, I read as much as I could on my own. Somewhere in there I learned something. I remember reading this from Sinclair Lewis at an early age:

"There are two insults no human will endure--the assertion that he has no sense of humor and the doubly impertinent assertion that he has never known trouble."

I've tried to stay away from sarcasm or fault-finding humor. It's becoming more common these days. It's a form a humor no one likes except, in some cases, the person who's dealing it out.

But humor--rightly used--can be a great remedy for what's wrong with the world. Try to find it in your associates and you'll never be sorry. Besides, your life will be a lot more enjoyable.

There's the old saw about "your reputation preceding you" and it's still true today.

Reputation is the one Quality Factor you have to depend mostly on others to supply. And believe me, they'll supply it, whether you want them to or not. Who was it who said, "Reputation is what you seem to be like"?

Whether or not your reputation is accurate, or

partly accurate or completely false, matters little. You're stuck with it, and you'll have a hard time shaking it from following you wherever you go.

Sure, you can change your reputation. But the old reputation keeps hanging around. The bits and pieces of what you used to be keep showing up at the worst possible times. All of us need to know that we can easily lose what we've spent years in building by just one poor or not-thought-through move.

And remember, most people remember the bad much more easily than the good!

The other thing I've noticed about reputation is that a lot of people work hard to get theirs early, then want to coast on it for the rest of their lives, or maybe coast on their family's reputation.

It's not to be. More than a hundred years ago, Alvan Macauley wrote this:

"We sometimes speak of winning reputation
as though that were the final goal.
The truth is contrary to this.
Reputation is a reward,
to be sure,
but it is really the beginning,
not the end of endeavor.
It should not be the signal for a let-down,
but rather, a reminder that the standards
which won recognition can never
again be lowered.
From him who gives much--much is
forever after expected."

There are two other words that go hand-in-hand with reputation. They are character and credibility, the latter a term much used and abused in recent years. Credibility, in fact, is truth and reputation for truth.

I think it was my Dad who quoted someone saying: "One good thing about telling the truth, Freddie. You don't have to remember what you said."

He was right. <u>Truth is not always popular, but it is always right. And reputation, a good one, always walks with truth.</u>

Good character is a bit closer, in my opinion, to having a good reputation. Somebody once said, "Reputation is what you need to get a job; character is what you need to keep it." I firmly believe if you take care of your character your reputation will take care of itself.

My brother Charles was never known as a moralist although at times he may have thought of himself as one. At any rate, he was always free with his advice, and really quite often, he came up with a winner. One time I was asking him about a job application I was having trouble with.

He said, "Freddie, don't worry about references. You don't have any they're interested in. Just tell them your past is clean and good and filled with work, and that's the best reference they could have that you'll be good in the future."

By all means check the reputations of people you're going to be associated with. You can't do too much of this. Double and triple check. Get third and fourth opinions.

It's a lot easier to handle all this before than at a later shouting session.

Remember, what other people think of your associate-to-be is important; not final decision important, but important.

Ambition is a wild stallion all of us should ride at some point in our lives. Let's just hope we don't have to ride it off the cliff.

I define ambition as the everlasting drive to be

first. We hope it results in accomplishment, and, even more to be desired, that accomplishment is good.

If we do equate ambition and accomplishment, at least at the start, then let me bring to you something else the Bosselman family has tried to practice over the years:

Every accomplishment, small or large, has to start with the words, "I'll try."

There is the great benefit of ambition. It simply means that nothing is too big for an ambitious person. No fear. No excuses. No stopping once started. It's a marvelous character trait, despite what some historians have said.

In Caesar's time ambition often was described as greed. Brutus, Mark Antony said at the funeral oration, killed Caesar because of Caesar's ambition.

Throughout ancient history we find this same attitude--that ambition ruins man. I suppose this "too ambitious" description became a good way to keep people from advancement and self-improvement. About the time man became free to enjoy a few fruits of his labor, and was free from the tryanny of his fellow man, then ambition became a good word.

It was okay to try to come in first. It was okay to become a top dog. By the time my ancestors arrived in America in the 1860's, ambition was the single most important word of the day.

They proved a fact I've always thought was true--whether you're trying to settle a frontier or to fire up a dissatisfied worker--*people are never truly happy unless they are striving for something they believe is worth their time and effort. Think about that one for a bit!*

If you can spur someone's ambition with a worthwhile goal, then you'll have worthwhile associates.

When we were on the farm near Worms in my teenage years and my Dad became sick and unable to work, there was a huge extra burden on Charles, Norman and me just to keep that farm going. We did that. But it's the extra things we did that really made us proud.

Cash was always short in those days--something like it is today. One winter my brother Norman and I figured we could make some extra money trapping animals on the nearby Loup River. We set our lines along eight miles of the Loup and took turns running them. Believe me, it was cold up there, particularly at four in the morning when we hiked the upstream half of the line.

We had a tent, some blankets, a gas lantern which supplied heat--plus a lot of ambition. Actually, we did fine. Our catches multiplied by the week as we got the hang of it.

I remember one time we got a badger. We had no idea what a badger pelt was worth. We skinned it and sent it in along with the others and surprise, back came $18 for that skin alone. We thought we had found a gold mine. We never did get another badger, but we lived on enthusiasm alone for another few weeks--just enough to add substantial money to our meager cash pile.

The point here is that if you want or need something badly enough, you'll always find a way to get it.

<u>That's a Quality Factor you want to discover in others.</u>

Ambition often leaves scars. Every success probably leaves marks made by obstacles and competitors, so don't expect untouched virginity in your ambitious associates. Just look for those sometimes scarred ones who still have the drive and the will power to succeed.

When you're dealing with people always remember you're not dealing in logic. As Dale Carnegie said, you're dealing "with creatures of emotion, creatures bristling with prejudice and motivated by pride and vanity." He did well by appealing to those basic instincts.

Until recent years, my life has always been a

struggle. But I liked that; I liked work and I loved my family. The rest was important--the people, the challenges , the recognition--though not as important as the love and concern I held for those closest to me. You, too, will have to set your priorities, as you study the priorities set by your associates whom you've hopefully picked through the Quality Factors.

Thomas Edison once said: *"The three great essentials to achieve anything worthwhile are, first, hard work; second, stick-to-itiveness; third, common sense."*

I have a hard-and-fast rule I always use when someone recommends a person to me. I may agree that we need this particular talent. I may agree the candidate is personable, has a good sense of humor, is honest, has a good family and reputation and is ambitous.

But I always ask, "Does he know how to work?"

INDEX